Jewish
Roots of
Christianity

© 2021 by Southwest Radio Church of the Air. All rights reserved. No part of this book may be used or reproduced in any manner whatsoever without written permission of the publisher, except in the case of brief quotations in articles and reviews. For more information contact:

Beacon Street Press
500 Beacon Drive
Oklahoma City, OK 73127
1-800-652-1144
www.swrc.com

Printed in the United States of America

ISBN 1-933641-61-4

To
John & Janice! 4/10/22

Jewish *Roots of* Christianity

Larry Stamm

In loving memory of my good friend Daryl,
who went to be with the Lord in 2014.
He was my primary mentor early in my walk with the Lord
and rejoiced with me as I began to make
connections between my Jewishness and Jesus.
Being an avid reader,
Daryl would have been thrilled to receive this book.

Also by Larry Stamm

Serving In His Court
Biblical Principles for Personal Evangelism
from the Heart of a Coach
Available from swrc.com

Into the Gale
Twelve Evangelistic Lessons from the Book of Acts
Available from swrc.com

Acknowledgments

First and foremost, I want to thank my Lord and Savior Jesus, who is my life and in whom I live, breathe, and have my being. A huge thank you goes out to my beautiful and supportive wife Lori. In addition to being my partner in life and best friend, she's also my greatest champion and partner in ministry.

Many thanks to Dr. Kenneth Hill and Matthew Hill for their friendship, partnership in ministry, and support of this project!

Also, thank you to my friends at Southwest Radio Ministries and Beacon Street Press, who championed the writing of the book and brought the project to fruition. Also, a big thank you to Christi Killian, my editor and graphic artist. Additionally, much appreciation goes out to Edie Rhodes, who spent many hours proofreading the manuscript. Their professional expertise and support were tremendous and helped make this project possible.

Finally, to the many people and churches who've sown into my spiritual life throughout the years, thank you for investing in me and in eternity.

Contents

Introduction 9

1. According to the Scriptures 20
2. Pillars of the Gospel 35
3. The Tapestry of Salvation 51
4. God's Covenants with Abraham and David 66
5. The Old Covenant Versus the New Covenant 82
6. Israel in Romans 9–11 98
7. The Temple, Tabernacle, and the Christian 113
8. Passover and Pentecost 128
9. The Fall Feasts of Israel 142
10. Messianic Prophecy: The Truth Is Out There! 157
11. The Trinity in the Old Testament 172
12. New Testament Applications 186

About The Author 201

Bibliography 208

Introduction

Christianity is Jewish! That statement is pregnant with meaning. What do I mean by that? That's what this book is all about. You see, I'm both Jewish and Christian.

Let me explain.

I grew up in a home that practiced Reform Judaism, a liberal expression of the faith. While we were culturally and socially very much connected to the Jewish community, we didn't have much of a religious and spiritual connection to the God of Israel. Yet, I received religious training, and from the time I could remember, I always believed in God and believed He knew me and saw me as special in some way.

I was bar mitzvahed just prior to my thirteenth birthday. *Bar mitzvah* is Hebrew and means "son of the commandment." It's a ceremonial rite of passage when a Jewish boy becomes a man, and yes, my family was very proud of me. For many young people in the Reform tradition, this highlight culminates religious training, and so it was for me also.

In high school I drifted from my religion and embraced athletics and academics. As a state-ranked tennis player in Florida and an honor roll student, I sought fulfillment and affirmation through achievement. However, those things didn't bring fulfillment. They left me wanting.

Introduction

As a follower of Jesus, I see the reality that every human being has a God-shaped hole in his or her soul only the Lord Jesus can fill. In college, I sought to fill that God-shaped hole with the party scene and earthly pleasures, yet those things didn't meet the deepest need of my soul, namely the need to be forgiven and rightly connected to my Creator.

During those years at the University of Florida, people began coming into my life sharing their faith in Jesus Christ with me. However, Jesus was foreign to us in the unbelieving Jewish community. I say "unbelieving" because there actually are many Jewish people who do believe in Jesus as Messiah and Lord! I'll talk more about that later. I didn't want to hear about "their" Jesus. You see, he wasn't for "us."

In fact, a common perception of many unbelieving Jewish people today is that Jesus is simply the god of the Gentiles and has nothing to do with us as Jews. That was certainly my understanding as a youth. When I was growing up, we never spoke about Jesus in the synagogue, nor did we learn about Him at all in Hebrew school.

Interestingly, the Holy Spirit continued moving, and people kept coming into my life trying to tell me that Jesus is the promised Messiah of Israel, that He died for my sins and rose again, and that through faith in Him, I could be forgiven, reconciled to God, and experience abundant and eternal life. In no uncertain terms, my initial response to these overtures was an emphatic "No!" My background informed me that Jesus and being Jewish just didn't jive.

My perception about reality was soon to be attacked by a friend and fellow student, Greg. He was a Christian who shared his faith, but in ways no one had previously done. Unique to his approach was a challenge to my understanding of reality. Specifically, he made one "fantastic" statement and posed one "intimidating" question that rocked my world to the core of my being.

He said, "Larry, there's absolute truth, and you can get in touch with it." Then he asked, "Do you know where you came from, do you know who you are, and do you know where you're going when you die?"

I was stunned. Those words from my friend sent me spiraling into an existential crisis of sorts. You see, at that moment in time I didn't know how to even begin processing this idea of "absolute truth." At the same time, I couldn't begin answering his challenging questions about meaning and destiny. On some level, I knew I was a "lost soul." I was that person walking around in quiet desperation. I did not have a clue about absolute truth, and I certainly did not know who I was or where I was going when I died.

The Holy Spirit used Greg's challenging statement and questions as a catalyst. I did begin searching for truth. At that time, I didn't necessarily embrace Christianity, nor did I go back to my Jewish faith. But I started what you might call a conscious search for truth, examining different world views, philosophies, and religions. If there was such a thing as absolute truth, I wanted to know.

Let's fast forward on my journey. It's now September 1987, a year after I graduated from the University of Florida. I flew home to St. Petersburg, Florida, from Atlanta, where I had visited my sister. I sat on the airplane reading *The Story of Philosophy* by Will Durant. A gentlemen sat next to me, noticed the book, and stated, "A philosophy book. Are you interested in philosophy?"

"Yes," I said.

He happily responded, "Great, we have a lot talk about. I have a master's degree in philosophy."

At this point you may be wondering about the direction our talk took. Yes, he shared his faith in Jesus with me! He made a curious statement, then posed a compelling question that rocked my world again, but in an inviting, not an intimidating way.

His name was Steve, and he was a traveling insurance salesman from Owensboro, Kentucky.

Steve said, "I've tried sex, drugs, and rock-n-roll, but who I've ended up with is Jesus!" I thought those were strange words. *Who?* I wondered. Then he said, "It's not a religion. Rather, I have a relationship with the living God." Then the question that changed my life came forth from his lips. "You tell me you're Jewish and believe in God. Then why don't you ask the God of Abraham, Isaac, and Jacob to show you the truth? Ask your God as you know Him if Jesus is the promised Messiah, and He'll show you the truth."

At this point on my journey, I was twenty-three years old, at the end of my proverbial rope, going nowhere fast. But there were not only the gospel seeds my friend Greg had sown and this man Steve was sowing. There were others as well on my journey that had been pointing me to Jesus. So I realized this divine appointment was not a coincidence, but providence. I told him, "I can do that. I can ask my God what the truth is."

Steve gave me his business card, wrote down some scriptures from the New Testament letters of Romans and Hebrews, and told me to call if I wanted, that he would be praying for me.

I got off the airplane that day and prayed a deep theological prayer. I said, "God, help! I'm not sure about Jesus, the Bible, Christianity, or the Messiah. But I believe you are real. If Jesus is the Messiah, show me."

God declared through the prophet in Jeremiah 33:3, "Call to Me, and I will answer you, and show you great and mighty things, which you do not know." The God of Abraham, Isaac, and Jacob answered my prayer powerfully and clearly!

Three months later in early December 1987, I called Steve on the phone and prayed to receive Jesus as my Lord and Savior. By God's grace I had become a Christian! As I began walking with the Lord Jesus and studying the New Testament as a young believer, I had an epiphany—Christianity is Jewish!

Why Didn't Anybody Tell Me This?

I'm the first believer in my family! In fact, I was what you might call a "closet Christian," as it took eighteen months for me to come out and tell my family about my faith in Jesus.

I'm a first-generation Holocaust survivor. My father and his family escaped Nazi Germany in May 1939. An SS agent in the Nazi Party, a friend of my grandfather who had fought with him in the German Army in World War I, falsified papers that enabled them to leave the country. They left Germany for British Honduras (present-day Belize), then immigrated to Daytona Beach, Florida, in 1941. I say that to reinforce my Jewish ethos. Culturally and socially, my Jewish identity hasn't left me because I'm now a follower of Jesus Christ. As I like to say, I'm not a converted Jew. I'm a converted sinner. Rather, I'm a completed Jew. And the most "Jewish" thing I, or anyone, could do is to place their trust in the Jewish Messiah and Savior of the world, Jesus.

The very first Jewish believer in Jesus I met was a long-time friend of our family, a woman named Myrna. After I shared my faith with my mom, she encouraged me to go to church with Myrna and her husband Al. Before I declared my new-found faith to my mom, I had no clue Myrna was a Christian. I first began attending church with Myrna and Al in 1989. As I began studying the New Testament and learning about the faith, I gained understanding about things of which I previously was ignorant. Jesus was Jewish. That I knew. What I didn't know was that the disciples, including Peter, James, and John, were all Jewish, and that all the writers of the New Testament, with the possible exception of Luke, were Jewish.

I came to understand that in one sense the gospel accounts are simply a Jewish debate among Jewish people about the true identity of a Jewish man, Jesus. The story takes place in the Holy Land, Israel. Now, what could be more Jewish than that! Why didn't anybody tell me this while I was growing up?

Connecting the Dots

In 1991, the Lord brought me to Tennessee. At the time, I was a tennis coach at clubs and academies, but wanted to get into college tennis, as colleges tennis coaches have more time off than club and academy coaches. Frankly, I was burned out. I loved coaching but didn't love the hours I was working. In the fall of 1991, I moved from Florida to Tennessee and became an assistant tennis coach at East Tennessee State University.

My first exposure to "Jewish roots" teaching occurred in the early 1990s. A woman I went to church with gave me a cassette tape set from the Institute of Jewish Christian Studies. They were a ministry that "connected the dots" between the Old Testament and New Testament, the instructors themselves were messianic Jews, Zola Levitt and Dr. Jeffrey Seif. As I immersed myself in this teaching, I was able to go back to my youth and make connections with my Jewish education in Hebrew school. Bible stories I learned and scriptures from the Old Testament I memorized as a youngster were being illuminated in a whole new light—the person and work of Messiah Jesus. This excited me.

At the same time in East Tennessee in the 1990s, the Holy Spirit began giving me a desire to share the gospel with my Jewish people, but there weren't many Jewish people in East Tennessee. A small men's prayer group from church I met with weekly in the mid-1990s began praying with me that the Lord would guide me and open a door of ministry to my Jewish people. In 1997, the Lord answered that prayer as He brought me out of coaching into full-time vocational ministry with Jews for Jesus, the preeminent mission preaching the gospel to my Jewish people.

I did two tours of ministry with Jews for Jesus. From 1997 to 1999, I played guitar and sang with the mobile evangelistic music team, called the Liberated Wailing Wall, while also doing a lot of street evangelism. During this time, I met and married my wonderful wife Lori, who was also serving at the ministry. Then, from 2003 to 2009, I was a front-line missionary in New York City evangelizing and discipling Jewish people and sharing the gospel with anyone willing to hear about Messiah.

Telling my Jewish people about Jesus meant helping them understand it was and is "kosher" to be Jewish and believe in Jesus. Primary to that effort was making connections between the Jewish scriptures (aka the Old Testament or Hebrew Bible) and Jesus. What a joy it was and is see lights go on, connections made, and professions of faith in Messiah happen!

What Is Jewish Roots?

In my journey to faith in Jesus, I didn't step inside the walls of a church, get exposed to the gospel on radio, television, or the Internet, or attend a Bible study. In short, I came to a saving knowledge of Jesus through the faithful testimony of Christians in the "marketplace"—which I define as anywhere outside the walls of a church.

After serving with Jews for Jesus, I served from 2009 to 2013 as a local outreach and missions pastor at our home church in Johnson City, Tennessee. In 2013, my wife Lori and I began Larry Stamm Ministries, a ministry that exists *to make the gospel of Jesus a confident topic of conversation for every Christian*. The Lord has given me a passion to help you, the believer, more effectively share the gospel with everyone in your sphere of influence. You can learn more about our ministry at larrystamm.org. And if you're reading this and haven't yet put your trust in Jesus, I pray this book will help you better understand what that means.

The two main pillars of our ministry are evangelism equipping and teaching Jewish roots of Christianity! What do Jewish roots and evangelism have to do with one another? Primarily, we teach Jewish roots to help build what we call gospel foundations. In other words, as we better understand the gospel, we will be able to share the gospel more effectively with others.

For the Christian, the material in this book flows out of a "Jewish Roots of Christianity" seminar I developed by God's grace and through His Spirit. I have been teaching this at churches and conferences since 2013.

For our purposes I want to define Jewish roots of Christianity. What is Jewish roots? In short, it the biblical panorama of redemptive history from Genesis to Revelation. This Jewish roots study will be a biblical survey whereby we introduce connections between biblical Judaism and Christianity, biblical Judaism being the religion of the Old Testament. We will be connecting the dots between the Old and New Testaments. In other words, this is a biblical exercise in how we got to here from there!

Perhaps you've heard this pithy catchphrase that packs a

punch: "The Old Testament is the New Testament concealed, and the New Testament is the Old Testament revealed." In short, we'll better understand the New Testament when we also study the Old Testament concurrently, and vice versa, for this is the whole counsel of God. Additionally, a foundation of biblical understanding and interpretation is that we better understand a text in the context in which it was written. In a grand sense, the text of the New Testament is in context of the Old Testament. Why and how? In short, that is the purpose of this book.

Here's a good starting point: Our Christian faith comes out of biblical Judaism, or the faith of Old Testament saints. Jesus said in Matthew 5:17, "Do not think that I came to destroy the Law or the Prophets. I did not come to destroy but to fulfill." So, in one sense Jesus is the fulfillment of biblical Judaism, the religion of the Old Testament!

Why study Jewish roots? My prayer is that our study will help you grow in your relationship with Jesus, gain a deeper understanding of the scriptures, and better understand, appreciate, and articulate the gospel. The Apostle Paul elucidated the goal of the gospel in Romans 1:16–17, "For I am not ashamed of the gospel of Christ, for it is the power of God to salvation for everyone who believes, for the Jew first and also for the Greek. For in it the righteousness of God is revealed from faith to faith; as it is written, 'The just shall live by faith.'"

This book is introductory in nature. In short, it is selective, not exhaustive. For example, when we study the Abrahamic covenant, we won't delve into circumcision, the sign of the covenant. We could do a deep-dive study into the "circumcision of the heart" the Apostle Paul wrote about in several New Testament passages with which you may be familiar. Surprisingly, in the Old Testament, God also spoke of the "circumcision of the heart." For the limited scope of our study, we'll omit this concept. Our study will be selective in nature. Additionally, I'll be providing a wealth of solid material in the recommended resource list at the end of the book to enhance your further study on any of the topics we will touch upon and explore.

We are about to embark on a journey down redemption road. As we travel through the Word of God, we'll pass by some really fascinating and important aspects. At some points, we may stop and briefly examine points of interest. At other places, we may stop and take a deeper, more critical look at the wonder of God's salvation plan found in Messiah Jesus. If you've ever traversed a scenic parkway with fantastic overlooks, you realize the majestic nature of the view, while also realizing there is so much more. Such is the nature of our study. We are just touching upon the panorama of God's redemptive plan. I trust it will be encouraging, edifying, and enlightening.

As we study, my heart's desire and prayer to God is that His Word will accomplish in your life all He desires and designs for you, and that you would better understand His plan of salvation and grow closer to the Savior.

> For as the rain comes down, and the snow from heaven, And do not return there, But water the earth, And make it bring forth and bud, That it may give seed to the sower And bread to the eater, So shall My word be that goes forth from My mouth; It shall not return to Me void, But it shall accomplish what I please, And it shall prosper in the thing for which I sent it.
> —Isaiah 55:10–11

Just as the splendor of a newborn baby elicits joy in a parent, my hope is that the discovery of all the myriad connections we'll uncover in this book will evoke awe, wonder, and praise to our great God!

The gospel is as deep as it is wide, and our understanding of the good news is never exhausted. This is the nature of God's Word in general, and the person and work of Jesus specifically. In short, this side of glory we will never arrive in knowing the riches of His grace, yet we study to show ourselves approved by God. We also study the gospel to share it more effectively with others.

I trust you will glean much from this work for His glory and your good. Understand that I will refer to a limited amount of scripture to make teaching points. Our study is a simple survey. Important, yes. Profound, yes, yet limited in nature. I refer to and provide recommended resources at the end of this volume that will enhance further study on various topics we shall endeavor to explore. My ultimate goal is simply that your faith will grow, as "… faith comes by hearing, and hearing by the word of God" (Romans 10:17).

Let's begin our journey!

Chapter 1

According to the Scriptures

A road atlas is awesome. Before the advent of such technological cyber-marvels as Mapquest and Googlemaps, I thoroughly enjoyed utilizing the road atlas on road trips. In the 2000s while a missionary with Jews for Jesus, I embarked every spring on a three-week national speaking tour in a selected region of the country, doing a visual sermon in churches entitled "Christ in the Passover."

I confirmed meeting details with churches, printed the Mapquest directions, and with my trusted atlas traversed from meeting to meeting. Today, I can get lost studying maps, enjoying the vast amount of information they provide, while at the same time pondering with joy all the adventures one could have going from place to place.

We begin our journey on redemption road in the Word of God, our "atlas," with the end in mind. What is the end? It's the person and work of Jesus.

In the midst of the Information Age and advent of twenty-first century technology, we are bombarded with messages daily. It takes work to sift through the messages and determine what to ignore, what is important, and what to act upon. Yet one message is singular, transcendent, powerful, and life changing. Amid the noise and clutter of a message-saturated world, it is simply the most important message of all.

What is that message? It is the gospel, the good news about Jesus. In fact, it is the very best news! The gospel is about Jesus' life and what He accomplished on our behalf. Namely, He paid our sin debt, providing a means of forgiveness, so that through faith in Him we can be reconciled to God and receive the gift of abundant and eternal life.

The gospel message is as deep as it is wide. It is the topic of volumes and volumes of books. For our purposes, we will touch on just some of the basics of the gospel message. While this entire book is about the gospel found in the person and work of Messiah Jesus, we're only touching highlights of God's glorious redemption found in Him. The topic is that immense. We should continually study the profundity of the gospel and its eternal implications.

In 1 Corinthians 15:3–4 the Apostle Paul articulated the foundation of the gospel message: "For I delivered to you first of all that which I also received: that Christ died for our sins according to the Scriptures, and that He was buried, and that He rose again the third day according to the Scriptures." Paul wrote to the church in Corinth that Christ died for our sins, was buried, and rose again "according to the scriptures." Of what scriptures was he speaking? The Old Testament!

When Paul wrote this first letter to the Corinthian church, the New Testament canon had not yet been compiled into one volume. While all twenty-seven books of the New Testament were written in the first century, copies of each into one known volume would have followed their writing. Hence, the "scriptures" was a reference to the Old Testament, also known as the Hebrew Bible, Jewish Bible, or Jewish Scriptures.

The most recent historical Old Testament book, Nehemiah, was penned about 400 B.C. at the latest. The remainder of the Old Testament canon was written prior to Nehemiah. Between 250 and 200 B.C., the Septuagint, a popular Greek translation of the Old Testament, was produced, which included the entire canon of the Old Testament. This critical use of the term "scripture" will help shape our understanding as we study God's Word. For example, when Jesus said, "It is written," He was referring to the Old Testament. Similarly, when we read in the New Testament "as the scripture says," this is also a reference to the Old Testament canon.

Paul elucidated the foundations of the gospel, stating that Christ died for our sins and rose again according to the scriptures. Note the three components:

1. Christ died for our sins—that's substitutionary atonement;
2. Christ rose again on the third day—that's resurrection; and
3. according to the scriptures—that's the Old Testament.

Therefore, we ought to be able to find both the principles of substitutionary atonement and resurrection in the Hebrew scriptures. We will as we further explore these pillars of gospel truth.

Before we explore the gospel in the Old Testament, let's witness Jesus' testimony of Himself according to the scriptures.

Jesus Testified from the Scripture

It was a dark, depressing moment in time. On the road to Emmaeus, two disciples were walking in despair, discussing the crucifixion of Christ. In their minds, it was a disaster.

In the account found in Luke 24, Jesus had already been crucified and resurrected. Then He met these disciples, Cleopas and an unidentified person, as they walked to the small town of Emmaus, not far from Jerusalem. "And they talked together of all these things which had happened. So it was, while they conversed and reasoned, that Jesus Himself drew near and went with them. But their eyes were restrained, so that they did not know Him" (Luke 24:14–16).

After Cleopas shared with Jesus about how they had heard the testimony of the angels to the resurrection and the women's testimony of the empty tomb, the Lord rebuked them, then testified of Himself from the scriptures: "Then He said to them, 'O foolish ones, and slow of heart to believe in all that the prophets have spoken! Ought not the Christ to have suffered these things and to enter into His glory?' And beginning at Moses and all the Prophets, He expounded to them in all the Scriptures the things concerning Himself" (Luke 24:25–27).

In John 5:38–40, Jesus rebuked people who believed in the scripture but not His testimony, "But you do not have His word abiding in you, because whom He sent, Him you do not believe. You search the Scriptures, for in them you think you have eternal life; and these are they which testify of Me. But you are not willing to come to Me that you may have life."

There are many other times Jesus witnessed of Himself from the Old Testament. When you study the New Testament, note the various places the Lord said, "It is written" or "according to the prophet ..." These are just two brief examples.

Defining Our Terms

As we begin our study of Jewish roots, it's helpful to define some commonly used terms that will enhance our understanding.

We've already mentioned different names for the Old Testament, like the Hebrew Bible or Jewish Scriptures. You may not realize, but unbelieving rabbis and the religion of Judaism categorically reject the New Testament as truth and Jesus as Messiah. The New Testament may also be referred to as "New Covenant"—*B'rit Chadashah* in Hebrew. The word *B'rit* means covenant, while the word *Chadashah* means "new."

The Hebrew word *besorah tovah* means "glad tidings" or "good news," from which we get the word "gospel"—in Greek *evangelion*. Note that the Old Testament was written mostly in Hebrew with these exceptions: a few chapters in the prophecies of Ezra and Daniel, and one verse in Jeremiah were written in Aramaic.[1] The New Testament was written in Koine Greek.

The name "Jew" originally derived from the tribe of Judah but was later ascribed to anyone who made up the southern kingdom of Judah. As you may remember, in the book of Genesis, Abraham begat Isaac and Isaac begat Jacob. God changed Jacob's name to Israel in Genesis 32:28: "And He said, 'Your name shall no longer be called Jacob, but Israel; for you have struggled with God and with men, and have prevailed.'" Eventually, the term became a distinction of any descendant of the twelve tribes of Jacob (Israel).

The term "gentile" derives from the Hebrew word *goyim*, meaning "nations." Gentile simply refers to a non-Jewish person.

Every person is either Jewish or gentile. As I like to say in teaching settings, knowing the Lord isn't about your Jewishness or gentileness—it's about your Jesusness! Do you know Him? And in similar fashion, I like to say that God's redemptive plan is not exclusively for Jews or gentiles—it's for mankind. For God so loved *the world!*

---

1. https://www.biblica.com/resources/bible-faqs/in-what-language-was-the-bible-first-written/

Speaking of redemption, it is the common theme running throughout the Bible, and our focus is our Redeemer Jesus. In the Old Testament, redemption was primarily deliverance out of physical slavery, as the Israelites were redeemed out of Egypt. In the New Testament, redemption primarily refers to deliverance from spiritual slavery, namely sin. As we'll discover in this study, we'll find redemption from sin all throughout the Word of God.

The word "redeem" literally means "to buy out." It was a term used specifically in reference to the purchase of a slave's freedom—that's physical redemption. The application of the term to Jesus' death on the cross is spiritual in nature. A person's spiritual condition prior to receiving Jesus by faith is that of a slave, a slave to sin. This is spiritual bondage. God has purchased our freedom through the shed blood of Christ, and as we trust in Him, we're no longer in bondage to sin. For example, the Apostle Paul referred to spiritual redemption accomplished by Jesus in Galatians 3:13, "Christ has redeemed us from the curse of the law, having become a curse for us (for it is written, 'Cursed is everyone who hangs on a tree')" and in Galatians 4:4–5, "But when the fullness of the time had come, God sent forth His Son, born of a woman, born under the law, to redeem those who were under the law, that we might receive the adoption as sons."

Interestingly, the words "Messiah" and "Christ" have a synonymous meaning, though derived from different languages. Both words mean "anointed one" or "chosen one." In Hebrew or Aramaic, the word is *Mashiach* from which we get Messiah, while in the Greek the word is *Christos*, meaning Christ. Once, while witnessing in a coffee shop to a fellow Jewish man with the same reform background as me, I noted that Christ and Messiah meant the same thing. He was blown away, never having heard the explanation. In short, while witnessing to a Jewish person, or anyone for that matter, don't assume they know the meaning of any "biblical terms." Whenever possible, explain terms so you can get on the same page.

In the Old Testament prophets, priests, and kings were anointed with oil to consecrate them for special service or to signify the endowment of God's Spirit (Leviticus 4:3; 8:12; 1 Samuel 10:1, 6; Psalm 105:15; Isaiah 61:1). For example, God told Elijah to anoint Elisha to succeed him as Israel's prophet in 1 Kings 19:16: "… And Elisha the son of Shaphat of Abel Meholah you shall anoint as prophet in your place."

Aaron was anointed as the first high priest of Israel in Leviticus 8:12: "And he poured some of the anointing oil on Aaron's head and anointed him, to consecrate him."

Samuel anointed David as king of Israel in 1 Samuel 16:13: "Then Samuel took the horn of oil and anointed him in the midst of his brothers; and the Spirit of the Lord came upon David from that day forward. So Samuel arose and went to Ramah."

All of these men held "anointed" positions, but the Old Testament predicted a coming Deliverer, chosen by God to redeem Israel. This Deliverer the Jewish people called "the Messiah," with a "capital M." He is referred to many times in the Jewish Bible, including Isaiah 61:1:

> The Spirit of the Lord God is upon Me,
> Because the Lord has anointed Me
> To preach good tidings to the poor;
> He has sent Me to heal the brokenhearted,
> To proclaim liberty to the captives,
> And the opening of the prison to those who are bound.
>
> —Isaiah 61:1

Additionally, the Messiah was to fulfill all three offices as the Prophet, Priest, and King! Jesus was and is a Prophet, Priest, and King. Moses told the Israelites to look for the Prophet in Deuteronomy 18:15, "The Lord your God will raise up for you a Prophet like me from your midst, from your brethren. Him you shall hear." As Hebrews 4:14 declares, "Seeing then that we have a great High Priest who has passed through the heavens, Jesus the Son of God, let us hold fast our confession." The Lord Jesus receives the glorious title of "King of Kings" in Revelation 17:14 and Revelation 19:16, among other places in the scripture.

John declared the purpose of his gospel in John 20:31, highlighting the messiahship of Jesus: "but these are written that you may believe that Jesus is the Christ, the Son of God, and that believing you may have life in His name."

Finally, the Hebrew name for Jesus is *Y'shua* or *Yeshua*, meaning "Yahweh saves" or "The Lord is salvation." The English spelling of the Hebrew *Yeshua* is "Joshua," but when translated from Hebrew into Koine Greek, the original language of the New Testament, the name Yeshua becomes *Iēsous*. In English, Iēsous becomes "Jesus." The name Jesus was quite popular in first-century Judea. For this reason, our Lord was often called "Jesus of Nazareth," distinguishing Him by His childhood home, the town of Nazareth in Galilee (Matthew 21:11; Mark 1:24; Luke 18:37; John 1:45; John 19:19; Acts 2:22).[2]

Biblical Judaism vs. Rabbinic Judaism

Biblical Judaism—according to the Scriptures
Rabbinic Judaism—according to the Scriptures and the rabbis

---

2. https://www.gotquestions.org/meaning-name-Jesus.html

Many Christians today are miffed about why so many Jewish people don't understand Jesus is the Messiah. Isn't the Bible clear about the issue? Yes, crystal clear, but that's not the problem. Both Christians and unbelieving Jewish people may be unaware of a huge problem that keeps the Jesus issue muddied for many in the Jewish community: the Judaism of Jesus' day is not the same as the Judaism of today. As we seek to glean understanding of the Jewishness of Jesus, this is one of the more important, yet often overlooked, dynamics that won't be overlooked, at least not in this book:

The Judaism of Jesus' Day Is Not the Judaism of Today!

This statement could be elucidated in a book (or several volumes). However, the "reader's digest" version I'll put forth will suffice for our purposes. Understand this reality and you'll understand so much, for this delineation will set the stage for the remainder of our discussion and study of Jewish roots. When we define terms, we create clarity and avoid confusion, and on the issue of Judaism and its relationship to Jesus, it's imperative to get it right!

First, let us declare that there is a great gulf fixed between biblical Judaism and rabbinic Judaism. Biblical Judaism is the religion of the Old Testament exclusively and finds its fulfillment in the person and work of Jesus, who said in Matthew 5:17, "Do not think that I came to destroy the Law or the Prophets. I did not come to destroy but to fulfill." Rabbinic Judaism, also called Orthodox or traditional rabbinic Judaism, is based on scripture, PLUS the traditions and teachings of the rabbis!

Biblical Judaism is the religion God gave Israel in the Old Testament and was based on the sacrificial system. Traditional rabbinic Judaism, also known as Orthodox Judaism today, is the religion the unbelieving rabbinic community developed following the destruction of the temple in A.D. 70. It's based on scripture plus tradition plus good works.

Let me explain. The two areas of greatest divergence between biblical Judaism and rabbinic Judaism are:

1. Whose word is authoritative—God's Word or man's word?; and
2. What is the means of forgiveness of sins.

Biblical Judaism declares that only God's Word, the Old Testament, is authoritative. The unbelieving rabbinic community thinks that the Holy Scriptures (the Old Testament) PLUS the teachings of the rabbis are authoritative. Those rabbinic teachings are found primarily in the Talmud (the oral law). The Talmud, the oral law, includes two parts:

1. the Mishnah (meaning "repetition" or "study"); and
2. the Gemara, which means "addition" or "completion."

Whereas the Mishnah barely cites biblical verses, for nearly every law discussed the Gamera introduces these connections between the biblical text and the practices and legal opinions of its time.[3]

Regarding the Talmud, the oral law, the Pharisees believed that on Mt. Sinai God not only gave Moses the written law, they believed God also gave Moses an oral law. This oral law was a companion, a supplement, an addition to the written law. The Pharisees also believed that Moses handed down this oral law to Aaron. Aaron passed it along to his sons, and then it was passed down orally

---

3. https://www.myjewishlearning.com/article/gemara-the-essence-of-the-talmud/

through the generations. By the time of Christ, these oral traditions had become authoritative in the religious paradigm of the Pharisees. That's why Jesus said six times on the Sermon on the Mount in Matthew 5, "You've heard it said, but I say unto you ..." Jesus was having to distinguish the law of Moses from the teachings of the Pharisees.

In another example, this oral tradition (also called the tradition of the elders) is rebuked by Jesus in Mark 7:5–9:

> Then the Pharisees and scribes asked Him, "Why do Your disciples not walk according to the tradition of the elders, but eat bread with unwashed hands?" He answered and said to them, "Well did Isaiah prophesy of you hypocrites, as it is written: 'This people honors Me with their lips, But their heart is far from Me. And in vain they worship Me, Teaching as doctrines the commandments of men.' For laying aside the commandment of God, you hold the tradition of men—the washing of pitchers and cups, and many other such things you do." He said to them, "All too well you reject the commandment of God, that you may keep your tradition.

Note that this oral tradition was codified or written down during the first five centuries after Christ into what we now call the Talmud, the oral law. This oral law is as authoritative in traditional rabbinic Judaism as is the Bible itself. And by the way, the Talmud is over twenty-five hundred pages and includes over three million words, so you can imagine the confusion this creates, especially when the Bible (the Hebrew scriptures) and the Talmud are at odds!

Perhaps that's why, on some level, God spoke these words to the Jewish people in Joshua 1:8: **"This Book of the Law shall not depart from your mouth, but you shall meditate in it day and night, that you may observe to do according to all that is written**

in it. For then you will make your way prosperous, and then you will have good success."

If you add the oral law to the Scriptures and add the commentaries of the rabbis throughout the generations to the milieu of religious authority, one can easily understand there is no coherent systematic theology in Judaism. At the end of the day, it simply depends on the rabbi.

Practically speaking, how does this work in a modern religious context? Here's a simple example. As a missionary in New York City for six years, when asking an Orthodox Jewish person what a particular passage in the Bible (the Old Testament) may mean, if he didn't know he would typically respond, "Let me ask my rabbi."

Hopefully I haven't confused you. In simple terms rabbinic Judaism is primarily about "deed" or doing, while Christianity is primarily about "creed" or believing.

The second great gulf fixed between biblical Judaism and rabbinic Judaism is the means of atonement. Under biblical Judaism, the altar of sacrifice was the means of atonement God gave Israel upon their inception. As Leviticus 17:11 declares, "For the life of the flesh is in the blood, and I have given it to you upon the altar to make atonement for your souls; for it is the blood that makes atonement for the soul."

In rabbinic Judaism, there was a huge obstacle that needed to be overcome following destruction of the second Temple in A.D. 70. Because there was no temple, there was no altar and no sacrifice. Hence, there was no forgiveness. But remember, at that time there was no longer a need for temple sacrifice because of the one-time atoning sacrifice of Jesus. As John the Baptist declared in John 1:29 about Y'shua (Jesus), "Behold! The Lamb of God who takes away the sin of the world!"

After the destruction of the temple, messianic Jews, those embracing Jesus as Messiah and Lord rejoiced while the unbelieving rabbinic community retreated into the desert to figure out how to propagate the religion of Judaism without the sacrificial system. The rabbinic community went to a city called Yavne in the Holy Land and founded a school of Jewish law. This school or counsel of Yavne is often understood as a wellspring of rabbinic Judaism. And it was here that the foundations of what we know today as traditional rabbinic Judaism or Orthodox Judaism were hammered out. Remember, the terms traditional rabbinic Judaism, rabbinic Judaism, and Orthodox Judaism are synonymous.

As an aside, until the nineteenth century this was the only Jewish religious expression. As a Jewish person, you were either secular or you were religious and followed Orthodox Judaism. In the nineteenth century, both Reform Judaism (a liberal expression) and Conservative Judaism (a balance between Reform and Orthodox Judaism) were developed and exist today. These are the three primary branches of Judaism in 2021. Today, only about ten to fifteen percent of the world's Jewish population are Orthodox. The remainder are Reform, Conservative, secular, or adhere to some "hybrid" expression of the faith.

Continuing our discussion on the origin of rabbinic Judaism, included in the tenets that stand today as definitive in traditional rabbinic Judaism is the means of forgiveness, which the Council of Yavne came to regard as efficacious. This magic formula for the forgiveness of sins became prayer plus repentance plus good works. One can find many scriptures for all these tenets in the Old Testament. However, there is a problem, a great fixed gulf.

God is the same yesterday, today, and forever. His ways don't change. Additionally, we must acknowledge that our sin debt must be paid. Here's an example I would use with Orthodox Jewish people with whom I was sharing the gospel.

Suppose I show up at the day of my arraignment, approach the judge, and say to him or her, "Your Honor, I did commit that crime (sin). I'm guilty as charged, but here's the deal. I've repented of that behavior (sin), I've given alms to the poor, and I'm really, really, really sorry. Can I go home now?"

How do you suppose the judge will respond? With derision! In so many words, that judge will say, "Sit down, and understand this—the debt must be paid."

We get it. Prayer, repentance, and good works are good and just, but they don't atone for sins!

Now that we've defined our terms, we can now begin unpacking the gospel as revealed in the Old Testament.

Chapter 1 Study Guide

1. What is the most important message in the world? What factors in life oppose our focusing on and sharing that message?
2. What is the scriptural foundation of the gospel in the New Testament?
3. According to 1 Corinthians 15:3–4, what are the three primary components of the gospel message?
4. When the Apostle Paul referred to the "scriptures" in 1 Corinthians 15:3–4, to what scriptures was he referring?
5. List the various names ascribed to both the Old Testament and New Testament that we noted in this chapter.
6. What did you learn about the name of Jesus that you may not have known before this survey?
7. Why do you think it's important to clarify definitions of biblical terms and concepts? Additionally, how do you think clarifying words and concepts with others may affect your gospel witness?
8. How did we define "redemption"? Why is the concept critical to our understanding of the gospel message and our evangelistic or witnessing efforts?
9. Compare and contrast the meaning of the words "Messiah" and "Christ." How are they alike, and how are they different? What difference might their usage have in your witness to people?
10. What are the two main differences between biblical Judaism and rabbinic Judaism? Why does it matter?

Chapter 2

Pillars of the Gospel

For an exhilarating week in June of 2015, I had the privilege of barnstorming through Honduras with an indigenous pastor friend named Louis while teaching at churches and at a seminary in Louis' hometown of Siguatepeque.

Honduras is a beautiful country with mountains in the center. During one long drive we stopped at a scenic overlook in the nation's capital of Tegucigalpa, a city of around a million people. From that overlook we could peer out for miles down into the valley, right into the heart of the city. However, just behind us on a hill were several large buildings, seemingly complete, but eerily unoccupied and off-kilter just a bit. When I asked Louis about them, he said they were unfit for occupation, as they were built upon an inadequate foundation. Had those buildings been erected upon a good foundation, they could have been useful, and occupied, with an incredible view people would have thoroughly enjoyed.

Foundations are important, not only in the physical realm, but also in the spiritual realm. A foundation is something such as an idea, a principle, or a fact that provides support for something. When applied to the spiritual realm, the person and work of Jesus is that foundation for the forgiveness of sins, the gift of abundant life, and eternal life. As we work through the foundations of the gospel message, that message centered around the person and work of Jesus, we continue our study with the end in mind as we connect redemptive dots.

As mentioned earlier, the Apostle Paul declared those foundations in 1 Corinthians 15:3–4, "For I delivered to you first of all that which I also received: that Christ died for our sins according to the Scriptures, and that He was buried, and that He rose again the third day according to the Scriptures."

What are those pillars of the gospel? They are substitutionary atonement—"Christ died for our sins"; resurrection—"and that He was buried, and that He rose again the third day"; and the Scriptures—"according to the Scriptures." Here in 1 Corinthians 15 is a reference to the Old Testament or Hebrew Scriptures. Therefore, we ought to be able to identify many Old Testament scriptures that reveal both substitutionary atonement and resurrection. Not surprisingly, that's what we'll discover.

Remember, for the believer in Jesus Christ, we certainly have the New Testament revelation which elucidates in clear detail the gospel of Jesus. Yet, through our exercise in "How did we get here from there?" we are going to build gospel understanding utilizing the Jewish Bible as well. And as we better understand the gospel, we'll be more effective in sharing it with others. As we've mentioned, we'll never exhaust or discover the full riches of the gospel as revealed in God's holy Word.

In verses three and four of 1 Corinthians 15, we find the concepts of substitutionary atonement, resurrection, and the Scriptures. We now embark on our study in the Old Testament, clearly discovering and exploring those concepts of substitutionary atonement and resurrection—"according to the Scriptures."

Substitution: The Blessing of God's Provision for Sin

God is a God of forgiveness, specifically, the forgiveness of sin. As followers of Jesus, we're familiar with the catchphrase, "His pain, our gain." Jesus, the sinless Lamb of God, took our sin debt in full on the cross, and we, through faith in Him alone, receive forgiveness of sin.

In the Garden of Eden, just after Adam and Eve rebelled against God, eating from the tree of the knowledge of good and evil, they did something some people today might consider "standard operating procedure," but back in the garden it was unprecedented.

What was it? They attempted to cover their sin and shame:

> So when the woman saw that the tree was good for food, that it was pleasant to the eyes, and a tree desirable to make one wise, she took of its fruit and ate. She also gave to her husband with her, and he ate. Then the eyes of both of them were opened, and they knew that they were naked; and they sewed fig leaves together and made themselves coverings.
>
> —Genesis 3:6–7

Those "coverings" were loin cloths or waist coverings, made of fig leaves. This was their feeble attempt to deal with their sin. This was an unacceptable covering for sin. In Genesis 3:21 God Himself provided a covering for them, this covering being acceptable to God: "Also for Adam and his wife the Lord God made tunics of skin, and clothed them." Those tunics of skins were skins of animals. Something biblically significant is in play here, which also has an important evangelistic application for the Christian today!

First, note the difference between the fig leaf covering of Adam and Eve versus God's provision of a covering consisting of an animal skin. We have to ask, "Why an animal skin? What was wrong, if anything, with the effort of Adam and Eve?" The animal skin points to the gospel pillar of substitution. Specifically, an animal dies, shedding its blood, but there's more. Adam and Eve, though judged, did not die in that moment. The Lord, in His grace, provided a substitute payment for their sin in the symbol of the animal skin, and in so doing communicated something profound and powerful.

Did the animal deserve to die? No. Adam and Eve did.

This concept of substitutionary atonement would be established by God when He birthed the nation of Israel, giving them the altar of sacrifice as the means of atonement: "For the life of the flesh is in the blood, and I have given it to you upon the altar to make atonement for your souls; for it is the blood that makes atonement for the soul" (Leviticus 17:11).

The whole of the Old Testament points toward the great sacrifice that was to come—that of Jesus' sacrificial giving of His own life on our behalf. Leviticus 17:11 is the Old Testament's central statement about the significance of blood in the sacrificial system.

A "sacrifice" is defined as the offering up of something precious for a cause or a reason. Making atonement is satisfying someone or something for an offense committed. Leviticus 17:11 can be read more clearly now. God said, "I have given it to you [the creature's life, which is in its blood] to make atonement for souls [covering the offense you have committed against Me]." In other words, those who are covered by the blood sacrifice are set free from the consequences of sin.[4]

While this concept of blood sacrifice is introduced and estab-

---

4. https://www.gotquestions.org/blood-sacrifice.html

lished in the Hebrew scriptures, it is reaffirmed in the New Testament through the death of Christ and the declaration of the Word of God itself. As Hebrews 9:22 declares, "… without shedding of blood there is no remission [forgiveness]." The Apostle Paul added in Ephesians 1:7, "In Him we have redemption through His blood, the forgiveness of sins, according to the riches of His grace."

From an evangelistic standpoint, the attempt of Adam and Eve to deal with their guilt symbolically represents a "works-based" attempt to deal with sin, whereas God provides His means of atonement, a covering for sin, through His provision.

One massive difference between those two basic approaches in dealing with mankind's "sin problem" is man's works-based approach versus God's provision. This points ultimately to the roads that lead to heaven. All religious systems promise an ultimate destination of heaven, paradise, or nirvana. Yet, there are only two ways to deal with sin—either through some combination of prayer, repentance, or good works man achieves enough to "get there" (a works-based system), or God does it all, providing the means of atonement.

It's man's effort versus God's provision. Biblical Christianity is based upon faith in God's provision, while all other religions, regardless of name, are based upon man's effort. It is either "do this" (man's effort) or "this happened" (Jesus did it all on the cross). These are the only two possible systems of forgiveness. This is the great gulf fixed between true and false religion, that is, true religion, the religion of the Bible, versus all other religious systems.

As you think about your witness for Jesus Christ, this dynamic difference we see in Genesis 3 should both inform and simplify your testimony to others. In this sense delineating between Christianity and all other religions is rather simple and straightforward.

That's why forgiveness is a gift. It can't be earned. As the Apostle

Paul wrote in Ephesians 2:8-9, "For by grace you have been saved through faith, and that not of yourselves; it is the gift of God, not of works, lest anyone should boast."

Messiah in the Levitical Offerings

There are five main types of sacrifices, or offerings, in the Old Testament. The burnt offering, the grain offering, the peace offering, the sin offering, and the trespass offering. Each of these sacrifices contained certain elements involving either an animal or fruit of the field. Additionally, each had a specific purpose. Most sacrifices were divided into two or three portions—God's portion, the portion for the Levites or priests, and, if there was a third, a portion kept by the person offering the sacrifice. The sacrifices can be generally categorized as either voluntary or mandatory offerings.

The chart below provides a basic overview of the Levitical offerings, which all point to the ultimate fulfillment found in the person and work of Messiah Jesus.

Offering	Messiah's Provision	Messiah's Character
Burnt Offering (voluntary)—Leviticus 1:3–17; 6:8–13	atonement	Messiah's sinless nature
Meal Offering (voluntary)—Leviticus 2:1–16; 6:14–23	dedication/ consecration	Messiah was wholly devoted to the Father's purposes

Peace Offering (voluntary)—Leviticus 3:1–17; 7:11–36	reconciliation/ fellowship	Messiah was at peace with God
Sin Offering (mandatory)—Leviticus 4:1–5:13; 6:24–30	propitiation	Messiah's substitutionary death
Trespass Offering (mandatory)—Leviticus 5:14–6:7; 7:1–10	repentance	Messiah paid it all for our redemption

For our purposes in this introductory survey, we'll only touch upon the sin offering, as it points directly to Jesus' sacrifice on the cross. As John 1:29 declares, "… Behold! The Lamb of God who takes away the sin of the world!"

Remember, the sacrifices in the Old Testament pointed forward to the perfect and final sacrifice of Messiah Jesus. As with the rest of the law, those sacrifices "… are a shadow of things to come, but the substance is of Christ" (Colossians 2:17).

The Sin Offering Keys

These are the sin offering keys—three things accomplished in Old Testament ritual sacrifice:

- » **Identification**—The offeror and offering are identified as one.
- » **Substitution**—The offering is on behalf of the offeror.

» **Exchange of life**—The offering dies, the offeror lives.

As an example, note the three keys of the sin offering found in Leviticus 4:27–31:

> If anyone of the common people sins unintentionally by doing something against any of the commandments of the Lord in anything which ought not to be done, and is guilty, or if his sin which he has committed comes to his knowledge, then **he shall bring as his offering a kid of the goats, a female without blemish, for his sin which he has committed. And he shall lay his hand on the head of the sin offering, and kill the sin offering at the place of the burnt offering.** Then the priest shall take some of its blood with his finger, put it on the horns of the altar of burnt offering, and pour all the remaining blood at the base of the altar. He shall remove all its fat, as fat is removed from the sacrifice of the peace offering; and the priest shall burn it on the altar for a sweet aroma to the Lord. **So the priest shall make atonement for him, and it shall be forgiven him.**

Substitution is made in verse 28, as an offering is made on behalf of the offeror, "he shall bring as his offering a kid of the goats, a female without blemish, for his sin which he has committed." Notice also that the offering is "without blemish."

We find identification and exchange of life in verse 29, "And he shall lay his hand on the head of the sin offering, and kill the sin offering at the place of the burnt offering." Notice the personal nature of identification, as the guilty party lays his hands on the head of the offering. In modern parlance, we might say, "That should be me!" Why? Because the innocent offering dies while the guilty party lives.

In verse 31, the transaction of the sin offering is complete, as atonement is made and the offeror is forgiven, "So the priest shall make atonement for him, and it shall be forgiven him."

Hallelujah for the Lamb of God

As Christians today we recognize the sacrificial death of Jesus on the cross as the only needed sacrifice for sin, offered once for all. As Hebrews 10:1–10 declares:

> For the law, having a shadow of the good things to come, and not the very image of the things, can never with these same sacrifices, which they offer continually year by year, make those who approach perfect. For then would they not have ceased to be offered? For the worshipers, once purified, would have had no more consciousness of sins. But in those sacrifices there is a reminder of sins every year. For it is not possible that the blood of bulls and goats could take away sins. Therefore, when He came into the world, He said: "Sacrifice and offering You did not desire, But a body You have prepared for Me. In burnt offerings and sacrifices for sin You had no pleasure. Then I said, 'Behold, I have come— In the volume of the book it is written of Me— To do Your will, O God.'" Previously saying, "Sacrifice and offering, burnt offerings, and offerings for sin You did not desire, nor had pleasure in them" (which are offered according to the law), then He said, "Behold, I have come to do Your will, O God." He takes away the first that He may establish the second. By that will we have been sanctified through the offering of the body of Jesus Christ once for all.

Thank the Lord for the provision of the Son of God, Jesus, "the Lamb of God who takes away the sin of the world!" (John 1:29).

The Superiority of Messiah's Sacrifice

As we ponder connecting the biblical dots between the Old and New Testament texts, the books of Leviticus and Hebrews are uniquely connected. Both the Old Testament book of Leviticus and the New Testament book of Hebrews deal with sacrifices and the priesthood in detail. Additionally, the book of Hebrews quotes from Leviticus more than any other Old Testament book. While the book of Leviticus introduces the sacrificial system and priesthood, the New Testament book of Hebrews argues for a better sacrifice and better priesthood found in the person and work of Messiah Jesus, as we'll explain.

The chart below provides comparison and contrast between Old Testament sacrifices and the sacrifice of Christ. The operative word to keep in mind when comparing them is "better," as the sacrifice of Christ is better in every way as compared to Old Testament sacrifices.

Old Testament Sacrifices Compared to Messiah's Sacrifice

Leviticus		**Hebrews**
1. Old Covenant (temporary)	Heb. 7:22; 8:6, 13; 10:20	1. New Covenant (permanent)
2. Obsolete promises	Heb. 8:6–13	2. Better promises
3. A shadow	Heb. 8:5; 9:23–24; 10:1	3. The reality

4. Aaronic priesthood (many)	Heb. 6:19–7:25	4. Melchizedekian priesthood (one)
5. Sinful priesthood	Heb. 7:26–27; 9:7	5. Sinless priest
6. Mortality of priesthood	Heb. 7:16–17, 23–24	6. Forever priesthood
7. Daily sacrifices	Heb. 7:27; 9:12, 25–26	7. Once for all sacrifice
8. Animal sacrifices	Heb. 9:11–15; 26; 10:4–10	8. Sacrifice of God's Son
9. Ongoing sacrifices	Heb. 10:11–14, 18	9. Sacrifices no longer needed
10. One-year atonement	Heb. 7:25; 9:12, 15; 10:1–4	10. Eternal propitiation

God's provision for that perfect high priest and perfect sacrifice in Messiah Jesus is the central message of Hebrews. To understand Hebrews, one must understand Leviticus and other Old Testament passages.

A key word in Hebrews is "better." The word "better" is found thirteen times in the epistle and attributed primarily to three things:

1. a better priesthood;
2. a better sacrifice; and
3. a better covenant.

Mankind's need for a perfect high priest and perfect sacrifice was evident and fulfilled in the person of Jesus through the New Covenant, which we'll explore in a Chapter 5.

As compared to the priesthood and sacrifices introduced in Leviticus, the priesthood and sacrifice of Messiah is better, as Hebrews 9:23–28 explains:

> Therefore it was necessary that the copies of the things in the heavens should be purified with these, but the heavenly things themselves with better sacrifices than these. For Christ has not entered the holy places made with hands, which are copies of the true, but into heaven itself, now to appear in the presence of God for us; not that He should offer Himself often, as the high priest enters the Most Holy Place every year with blood of another—He then would have had to suffer often since the foundation of the world; but now, once at the end of the ages, He has appeared to put away sin by the sacrifice of Himself. And as it is appointed for men to die once, but after this the judgment, so Christ was offered once to bear the sins of many. To those who eagerly wait for Him He will appear a second time, apart from sin, for salvation.

The Apostle Paul summed up well the substitutionary work of Messiah Jesus on our behalf in 2 Corinthians 5:21, "For He made Him who knew no sin to be sin for us, that we might become the righteousness of God in Him." Hallelujah!

Resurrection: The Blessing of God's Victory Over Sin and Death

While the sacrifice of Christ provided the sacrifice for sin, His resurrection emphatically brings forth complete victory over sin and death! Here are just a few references to resurrection in the Hebrew Scriptures:

- Daniel 12:1–2— "At that time Michael shall stand up, The great prince who stands watch over the sons of your people; And there shall be a time of trouble, Such as never was since there was a nation, Even to that time. And at that time your people shall be delivered, Every one who is found written in the book. And many of those who sleep in the dust of the earth shall awake, Some to everlasting life, Some to shame and everlasting contempt."
- Hosea 6:2—" After two days He will revive us; On the third day He will raise us up, That we may live in His sight."
- Psalm 16:10—" For You will not leave my soul in Sheol, Nor will You allow Your Holy One to see corruption."
- Job 19:25–26—" For I know that my Redeemer lives, And He shall stand at last on the earth; And after my skin is destroyed, this I know, That in my flesh I shall see God." (See also Isaiah 26:19, Ezekiel 37:14, Psalm 49:15, Hosea 13:14.)

In the New Testament, we find illustrations of this reality and understanding. Hebrews 11:17–19 reveals that Abraham believed in resurrection: "By faith Abraham, when he was tested, offered up Isaac, and he who had received the promises offered up his only begotten son, of whom it was said, 'In Isaac your seed shall be called,' concluding that God was able to raise him up, even from the dead, from which he also received him in a figurative sense."

Just before Jesus raised Lazarus from the dead in John 11, Martha and the Lord had a conversation that reveals her belief in resurrection:

So when Jesus came, He found that he had already been in the tomb four days. Now Bethany was near Jerusalem, about two miles away. And many of the Jews had joined the women around Martha and Mary, to comfort them concerning their brother. Now Martha, as soon as she heard that Jesus was coming, went and met Him, but Mary was sitting in the house. Now Martha said to Jesus, "Lord, if You had been here, my brother would not have died. But even now I know that whatever You ask of God, God will give You." Jesus said to her, "Your brother will rise again." **Martha said to Him, "I know that he will rise again in the resurrection at the last day."**

—John 11:17–24

What would compel Martha to say such a thing? It was her understanding of the Jewish scriptures, the Old Testament, that would have informed her faith and belief in resurrection.

Finally, note the Pharisees' belief in resurrection, during a showdown with Paul in Acts 23:6–8. As a background to this text, remember the Pharisees believed in the supernatural, angels, and resurrection, while the Sadducees didn't. During a moment when both groups were interrogating the Apostle Paul, we discover that this reality caused an unexpected conflict—with resurrection being the point of contention:

But when Paul perceived that one part were Sadducees and the other Pharisees, he cried out in the council, "Men and brethren, I am a Pharisee, the son of a Pharisee; concerning the hope and resurrection of the dead I am being judged!" And when he had said this, a dissension arose between the Pharisees and the Sadducees; and the assembly was divided. **For Sadducees say that there is**

no resurrection—and no angel or spirit; but the Pharisees confess both.

As we ponder resurrection in light of the Christian faith, we remember the words of Christ, who declared in John 11:25–26, "Jesus said to her, 'I am the resurrection and the life. He who believes in Me, though he may die, he shall live. And whoever lives and believes in Me shall never die. Do you believe this?'"

And because of the reality of resurrection, namely the resurrection of Jesus, we rejoice in God's victory that is our victory, through faith in Him,

> Now this I say, brethren, that flesh and blood cannot inherit the kingdom of God; nor does corruption inherit incorruption. Behold, I tell you a mystery: We shall not all sleep, but we shall all be changed—in a moment, in the twinkling of an eye, at the last trumpet. For the trumpet will sound, and the dead will be raised incorruptible, and we shall be changed. For this corruptible must put on incorruption, and this mortal must put on immortality. So when this corruptible has put on incorruption, and this mortal has put on immortality, then shall be brought to pass the saying that is written: "Death is swallowed up in victory." "O Death, where is your sting? O Hades, where is your victory?" The sting of death is sin, and the strength of sin is the law. But thanks be to God, who gives us the victory through our Lord Jesus Christ.
>
> —1 Corinthians 15:50–57

Chapter 2 Study Guide

1. What are the three pillars of the gospel message, as communicated by the Apostle Paul in 1 Corinthians 15:3–4?
2. What is the difference between how Adam and Eve covered themselves in Genesis 3:7 and how God covered them in Genesis 3:21? Why does it matter in relationship to the gospel, if at all?
3. When God established the nation of Israel, what did He provide as the means of atonement? What is the foundational scripture associated with His provision?
4. What is the "companion" verse in the book of Hebrews, noted in this chapter, which corresponds to Leviticus 17:11?
5. In a contemporary sense, how does the "effort" of Adam and Eve to deal with their sin compare with God's provision for sin, as it relates to mankind's "sin problem"? In short, what are the two primary ways people try to deal with their sin?
6. Based upon the two "strategies" for dealing with the sin problem of mankind as it pertains to a proper relationship with God, how would you explain the gospel to a person who thinks there are many ways to heaven, nirvana, or paradise?
7. According to Colossians 2:17, describe the difference between Old Testament sacrifices and the sacrifice of Christ.
8. What are the sin offering keys—three things accomplished in Old Testament ritual sacrifice?
9. In one word, compare the sacrifice of Christ to the Old Testament sacrificial system.
10. Based upon the material presented in the chapter, did you learn anything new about resurrection, and if so, what?

Chapter 3

The Tapestry of Salvation

The Cloisters, also known as the Met Cloisters, is a museum in Fort Tryon Park located in Washington Heights, Manhattan, New York City. The Cloisters specializes in European medieval art and architecture, with a focus on the Romanesque and Gothic periods.

While a missionary in New York City from 2003 to 2009, I once served as chaperone for our son, Elijah, and others from his school on a field trip to the Cloisters. Among the most popular attractions at the Cloisters, the medieval branch of the Metropolitan Museum of Art, is a set of tapestries depicting the hunt of the fabled unicorn. A tapestry is a piece of thick textile fabric with pictures or designs formed by weaving colored weft threads or by embroidering on canvas, used as a wall hanging or furniture covering. The exquisite tapestries depicting the hunt of the fabled unicorn presented incredible detail filled with a wealth of color. One aspect of the physical tapestry is that one side looks unsightly and unclear, while on the other side everything is clear, making sense!

The idea of the tapestry may also be used in reference to an intricate or complex combination of things or sequence of events. Such is the connection for our study of redemptive history found in the Word of God. In this chapter we'll connect threads of redemption between the Hebrew scriptures, the Old Testament, and the

New Covenant scriptures, better known to Christians as the New Testament. Remember that in one sense the Old Testament is the New Testament concealed, and the New Testament is the Old Testament revealed. In this chapter we'll explore the wonderful tapestry of God's salvation as presented in the Scriptures, connecting threads of truth that I trust will help you more clearly gaze upon the wonders of His salvation in Christ Jesus!

The Fifth Gospel

Isaiah 53 has been coined by some Bible scholars as "the fifth gospel." Nowhere else in the Old Testament do we find such a clear picture of the saving work of the Messiah. Herein is a powerful prophecy putting it all together.

Written some seven centuries before Christ, it is an incredibly powerful messianic prophecy. Contained therein we find the foundational concepts of substitutionary atonement and resurrection according to the Scriptures.

In Isaiah 53:4–6 we see the substitutionary atonement of the suffering servant:

> **Surely He has borne our griefs And carried our sorrows;** Yet we esteemed Him stricken, Smitten by God, and afflicted. But **He was wounded for our transgressions,** He was bruised for our iniquities; The chastisement for our peace was upon Him, And **by His stripes we are healed.** All we like sheep have gone astray; We have turned, every one, to his own way; And **the Lord has laid on Him the iniquity of us all.**

If we didn't know this was chapter and verse from the Old Testament, we might mistake this passage for a section of the New Testament, for it sounds so much like Jesus. And it is!

Once, while ministering to an unbelieving Orthodox Jewish man named Leon, I asked to play a little game. I told Leon to close his eyes and listen to my reading from the Bible, and then I had him guess if it was the New Testament or Old Testament, our Jewish Bible. After I read Isaiah 53, he adamantly stated this was the New Testament "propaganda" about Jesus. Upon my revelation, he was confused and panicky. Because, yes, it was about Jesus, but to Leon, from a very unlikely source!

In Isaiah 53:9–11 we find a clear allusion to resurrection:

> And **they made His grave with the wicked— But with the rich at His death,** Because He had done no violence, Nor was any deceit in His mouth. Yet it pleased the Lord to bruise Him; He has put Him to grief. When You make His soul an offering for sin, **He shall see His seed, He shall prolong His days,** And the pleasure of the Lord shall prosper in His hand. **He shall see the labor of His soul, and be satisfied.** By His knowledge My righteous Servant shall justify many, For He shall bear their iniquities.

How is it possible that the suffering servant, who is dead in verse 9, then goes on to "see His seed" in verse 10 and then sees the "labor of His soul" in verse 11? It's resurrection! The suffering servant must rise from the dead, and that's exactly what we witness in the person of Jesus Christ some seven centuries after this prophecy was penned!

Faith Is the Key

How people were saved during the time of the Old Testament before the time of Christ is a confusing question to some people. As believers in Jesus Christ, we understand clearly that "... by grace you have been saved through faith, and that not of yourselves; it is the gift of God, not of works, lest anyone should boast" (Ephesians 2:8–9).

But what about the saints of old, those who preceded the time of Christ Jesus? How were they saved? Just the same as New Testament era saints—by grace through faith in God!

Old Testament saints were saved by grace through faith in God's promise of the Messiah (Genesis 15:6; Romans 4:1–8, 13–25). New Testament saints are saved by grace through faith in God's provision of the Messiah (Romans 3:21–26; Ephesians 2:8–9). Faith is the key that unlocks the door of salvation.

Genesis 15:6 is our starting point, "And he [Abraham] believed in the Lord, and He accounted it to him for righteousness." Incredibly, when the Apostle Paul argued for the concept of justification by faith, he used Abraham as his illustration! In the New Testament, justification is an act of God whereby He pronounces a sinner to be righteous because of that sinner's faith in Christ. But it's fascinating that Paul used Abraham, an Old Testament saint, to argue his point.

Note Paul's elucidation of the goal of the gospel and means of salvation in Romans 1:16–17: "For I am not ashamed of the gospel of Christ, for it is the power of God to salvation for everyone who believes, for the Jew first and also for the Greek. For in it the righteousness of God is revealed from faith to faith; as it is written, 'The just shall live by faith.'" "The just shall live by faith" is a quote directly from Habakkuk 2:4 in the Old Testament.

In Romans 4, the Apostle Paul made it very clear that the Old Testament way of salvation was the same as the New Testament way, which is by grace alone, through faith alone. To prove this, Paul pointed us to Abraham, who was saved by faith: "... Abraham believed God, and it was accounted to him for righteousness" (Romans 4:3). Again, Paul quoted the Old Testament to prove his point—Genesis 15:6 this time. Abraham could not have been saved by keeping the law, because he lived over four hundred years before the law was given![5]

Paul continued in Romans 4:13–25:

> For the promise that he would be the heir of the world was not to Abraham or to his seed through the law, but through the righteousness of faith. For if those who are of the law are heirs, faith is made void and the promise made of no effect, because the law brings about wrath; for where there is no law there is no transgression. Therefore it is of faith that it might be according to grace, so that the promise might be sure to all the seed, not only to those who are of the law, but also to those who are of the faith of Abraham, who is the father of us all (as it is written, "I have made you a father of many nations") in the presence of Him whom he believed—God, who gives life to the dead and calls those things which do not exist as though they did; who, contrary to hope, in hope believed, so that he became the father of many nations, according to what was spoken, "So shall your descendants be." And not being weak in faith, he did not consider his own body, already dead (since he was about a hundred years old), and the deadness of Sarah's womb. He did not waver at the promise of God through unbelief, but was strengthened in faith, giving glory to God, and being fully convinced that what He had promised He was also able to perform. And therefore "it was accounted to him for righteousness." Now it was not written for his sake alone that it was imputed to him, but also for us. It shall be imputed to us who believe in Him who raised

---

5. https://www.gotquestions.org/Old-Testament-salvation.html

up Jesus our Lord from the dead, who was delivered up because of our offenses, and was raised because of our justification.

In Romans 4:6–8, Paul wrote that David was also saved by faith, where he quoted from Psalm 32:1–2:

> just as David also describes the blessedness of the man to whom God imputes righteousness apart from works: "Blessed are those whose lawless deeds are forgiven, And whose sins are covered; Blessed is the man to whom the Lord shall not impute sin."

In short, righteousness is "credited" or given to those who have faith in God—Abraham, David, and you and I, all share the same way of salvation.

In God's providence and provision, the blood of Christ was retroactively applied to all Old Testament saints, as Hebrews 9:15 states, "And for this reason He is the Mediator of the new covenant, by means of death, for the redemption of the transgressions under the first covenant, that those who are called may receive the promise of the eternal inheritance."

Thank God for justification by faith! We revel in Paul's declaration in Romans 3:21–25:

> But now the righteousness of God apart from the law is revealed, being witnessed by the Law and the Prophets, even the righteousness of God, through faith in Jesus Christ, to all and on all who believe. For there is no difference; for all have sinned and fall short of the glory of God, being justified freely by His grace through the redemption that is in Christ Jesus, whom God set forth as a propitiation by His blood, through faith, to demonstrate His righteous-

ness, because in His forbearance God had passed over the sins that were previously committed,

The Hall of Faith

Speaking of faith, the heroes of the faith are listed in the "hall of faith" chapter, Hebrews 11. It's here the writer again reinforced this essential concept of faith and how it is the key to knowing and pleasing God:

> **Now faith is the substance of things hoped for, the evidence of things not seen. For by it the elders obtained a good testimony.** By faith we understand that the worlds were framed by the word of God, so that the things which are seen were not made of things which are visible. By faith Abel offered to God a more excellent sacrifice than Cain, through which he obtained witness that he was righteous, God testifying of his gifts; and through it he being dead still speaks. By faith Enoch was taken away so that he did not see death, "and was not found, because God had taken him"; for before he was taken he had this testimony, that he pleased God. But **without faith it is impossible to please Him, for he who comes to God must believe that He is, and that He is a rewarder of those who diligently seek Him.** By faith Noah, being divinely warned of things not yet seen, moved with godly fear, prepared an ark for the saving of his household, by which he condemned the world and became heir of the righteousness which is according to faith.
> —Hebrews 11:1–7

It's interesting to note that Abel, Enoch, and Noah were not Jewish! They preceded God's covenant with Abraham and the birth of the nation of Israel. Additionally, they couldn't have been saved under that law, for the law had not yet been given. Obviously, they were saved by faith, as were all the other saints of old listed in Hebrews 11, such as Joseph, Moses, and Samson.

A Snake on a Pole

A snake, a pole, and Jesus. Is there a connection? To one unfamiliar with the Bible, the question may be perplexing, but to one familiar with the teachings of Jesus, there is a powerful connection.

Jesus was the master teacher! He often utilized word pictures to communicate truth. He also utilized the Word of God itself, often citing the Bible (the Old Testament) in communicating aspects of His life, identity, and ministry. On one occasion in the middle of the night, He shared gospel truth with a man utilizing a visual picture found in the Scriptures to communicate the gospel. In so doing, the Lord provided us some valuable lessons as we seek to effectively communicate the good news in our world today.

In John 3, a Pharisee named Nicodemus came to Jesus in the middle of the night, seeking to interact with the Lord. In the process, Jesus declared to Nicodemus the reality of the new birth, stating "… unless one is born again, he cannot see the kingdom of God" (John 3:3).

The narrative surrounding the new birth continues in John 3:4–10:

> Nicodemus said to Him, "How can a man be born when he is old? Can he enter a second time into his mother's womb and be born?" Jesus answered, "Most assuredly, I say to you, unless one is born of water and the Spirit, he cannot enter the kingdom of God. That

which is born of the flesh is flesh, and that which is born of the Spirit is spirit. Do not marvel that I said to you, 'You must be born again.' The wind blows where it wishes, and you hear the sound of it, but cannot tell where it comes from and where it goes. So is everyone who is born of the Spirit." Nicodemus answered and said to Him, "How can these things be?" Jesus answered and said to him, "Are you the teacher of Israel, and do not know these things?

Nicodemus, "the teacher of Israel" (John 3:10), is perplexed by Jesus' teaching.

In John 3:14–15, Jesus made a gospel connection for Nicodemus directly from the Torah: "And as Moses lifted up the serpent in the wilderness, even so must the Son of Man be lifted up, that whoever believes in Him should not perish but have eternal life."

The Lord's capacity to communicate in an economy of words is staggering. These words, pregnant with meaning, reveal much about Him and His saving work. In these two verses Jesus referred to Numbers 21:5–9, where God judged the Israelites for their disobedience, while at the same time providing a means of physical salvation from the judgment:

> And the people spoke against God and against Moses: "Why have you brought us up out of Egypt to die in the wilderness? For there is no food and no water, and our soul loathes this worthless bread." So the LORD sent fiery serpents among the people, and they bit the people; and many of the people of Israel died. Therefore the people came to Moses, and said, "We have sinned, for we have spoken against the LORD and against you; pray to the LORD that He take away the serpents from us." So Moses prayed for the people. Then the LORD said to Moses, "Make a fiery serpent, and set it on a

pole; and it shall be that everyone who is bitten, when he looks at it, shall live." So Moses made a bronze serpent, and put it on a pole; and so it was, if a serpent had bitten anyone, when he looked at the bronze serpent, he lived.

This powerful word picture provides a poignant teaching moment, as our Lord elucidated salvation by faith from a wilderness wandering narrative in the book of Numbers.

God Is the Savior

Humanity needs a Savior, for we all have sinned and fall short of God's glory. Apart from God's grace and mercy, we are hopeless and helpless to adequately deal with our sin apart from God, our Savior.

As Christians, we trust in Jesus as Lord and Savior. You might find it interesting that by doing a quick word study of "savior" in the Bible, you'll find a number of references to the word "savior" in the Old Testament. For example, the Lord declared Himself the Savior in passages like Isaiah 43:11, "I, even I, am the Lord, And besides Me there is no savior." Isaiah 45:15 says, "Truly You are God, who hide Yourself, **O God of Israel, the Savior!"**

David wrote about the Savior God in 2 Samuel 22:3, declaring, "The God of my strength, in whom I will trust; My shield and the horn of my salvation, My stronghold and my refuge; **My Savior,** You save me from violence."

While God is Savior in a physical sense, as in His saving Israel out of bondage in Egypt, He is also Savior in a spiritual sense, as we commonly understand as believers in Jesus. Since God is holy, He can't tolerate the presence of sin, and, unless He somehow cleanses us, we can't be cleansed of sin and forgiven. Those who are not cleansed, those who are not saved and forgiven, will be separated from God for all eternity. God's solution is to offer the perfect sacrifice, once and for all, to cleanse us of sin and reconcile us to Himself, providing forgiveness. This He did through the work of His Son, Jesus, on the cross.

Every human being needs a Savior because we cannot save ourselves; without Jesus, we're described as "... having no hope and without God in the world" (Ephesians 2:12). We need a Savior and thank God—He's provided one. Jesus' death and resurrection have provided the means of salvation, the forgiveness of sins and the gift of eternal life for all who would repent from their sin and receive by faith the Savior, Jesus!

A Place at the Table

When teaching Jewish roots content at conferences and at churches, I sometimes like to quip, "God's redemptive plan is not exclusively about Jews or gentiles; it's about mankind!" In the Old Testament, God has much to say about gentiles having a place at the table of redemption!

We've discussed earlier that all saints were and are saved by grace through faith. We can and should rejoice in the reality that, even in the Old Testament, God made a way for gentiles. In the Hebrew scriptures, the Old Testament, prophecy reveals that when the Messiah arrived, He would not only come to save Israel, He would come to be the Savior of the world: "I, the Lord, have called You in righteousness, And will hold Your hand; I will keep You and give You as a covenant to the people, As a light to the Gentiles" (Isaiah 42:6).

In Isaiah 49:6, we read: "Indeed He says, 'It is too small a thing that You should be My Servant To raise up the tribes of Jacob, And to restore the preserved ones of Israel; I will also give You as a light to the Gentiles, That You should be My salvation to the ends of the earth.'"

And in the future kingdom of the Messiah, the millennial reign of Christ, which we'll explore in coming chapters, the temple in Jerusalem will be a focal point of worship for all people, Jew and gentile alike, as Isaiah 56:6–7 declares:

> "Also the sons of the foreigner Who join themselves to the Lord, to serve Him, And to love the name of the Lord, to be His servants— Everyone who keeps from defiling the Sabbath, And holds fast My covenant— Even them I will bring to My holy mountain, And make them joyful in My house of prayer. Their burnt offerings and their sacrifices Will be accepted on My altar; **For My house shall be called a house of prayer for all nations."**

Psalm 117:1 states, "Praise the Lord, all you Gentiles! Laud Him, all you peoples!" In Romans 15:11, the Apostle Paul quoted this Old Testament verse to support his argument (Romans 15:7–13) that from the beginning of time, God's redemptive purposes would include all people!

God sent the prophet Jonah to preach to Ninevah, a gentile city (Jonah 3:5–10). Ruth, a Moabitess (Ruth 1:16), became a follower of the God of Israel and is actually in the genealogy of Jesus (Matthew 1:5). Make no mistake; God's redemptive plan for man has always included gentiles! Hallelujah!

Salvation Strings

As we conclude our study on the beautiful tapestry of salvation in the

Jewish Bible, I want to connect salvation concepts highlighting an Old Testament scripture chain that coincides with New Testament truth. These passages will reinforce the common thread of redemption we find throughout the word of God.

- » **Our sins separate us from God.** In Isaiah 59:2 the scripture states, "But your iniquities have separated you from your God; And your sins have hidden His face from you, So that He will not hear." In the New Testament, Colossians 1:21 declares, "And you, who once were alienated [of God] and enemies [of God] in your mind by wicked works, yet now He has reconciled."
- » **All have sinned.** Ecclesiastes 7:20 says, "For there is not a just man on earth who does good And does not sin." Romans 3:23 declares, "for all have sinned and fall short of the glory of God."
- » **The soul that sins shall die.** Ezekiel 18:4 says, ""Behold, all souls are Mine; The soul of the father As well as the soul of the son is Mine; The soul who sins shall die." While Ezekiel 18:20, soberly states, "The soul who sins shall die. ..." In the New Testament, Paul wrote in Romans 6:23 that "... the wages of sin is death, but the gift of God is eternal life in Christ Jesus our Lord."
- » **We can't be righteous through good works; it must be faith.** God rebuked ancient Israel for their religious hypocrisy, as they went through the external motions in Isaiah 64:6, "But we are all like an unclean thing, **And all our righteousnesses are like filthy rags;** We all fade as a leaf, And our iniquities, like the wind, Have taken us away." Remember, earlier we quoted Habakkuk 2:4 where the prophet wrote, "... the just shall live by his faith." A corresponding truth in the New Testament is found in Romans 3:20: "Therefore by the deeds of the law no flesh will be justified in His sight, for by the law is the knowledge of sin."

» **The only effacacious (or satisfactory/acceptable) sacrifice is the Messiah's death.** Isaiah 53:10 affirms this concept: "Yet it pleased the Lord to bruise Him; He has put Him to grief. When You make His soul an offering for sin, He shall see His seed, He shall prolong His days, And the pleasure of the Lord shall prosper in His hand." Romans 3:21–22 connects that truth from the Old Testament by stating, "But now the righteousness of God apart from the law is revealed, being witnessed by the Law and the Prophets, even the righteousness of God, through faith in Jesus Christ, to all and on all who believe. For there is no difference."

Thank God for His Son, who paid our sin debt in full, "In this is love, not that we loved God, but that He loved us and sent His Son to be the propitiation for our sins" (1 John 4:10).

As we ponder the wonderful tapestry of salvation God has woven through His Word, may we respond in praise to our great Redeemer:

> Bless the Lord, O my soul; And all that is within me, bless His holy name! Bless the Lord, O my soul, And forget not all His benefits: … The Lord is merciful and gracious, Slow to anger, and abounding in mercy. He will not always strive with us, Nor will He keep His anger forever. He has not dealt with us according to our sins, Nor punished us according to our iniquities. For as the heavens are high above the earth, So great is His mercy toward those who fear Him; As far as the east is from the west, So far has He removed our transgressions from us.
>
> —Psalm 103:1–2, 8–12

Chapter 3 Study Guide

1. What Old Testament scripture is referred to by some Bible scholars as the "fifth gospel?" Why the moniker?
2. In what verses in Isaiah 53 do we see the substitutionary atonement of the "suffering servant" (Messiah) along with the allusion to resurrection?
3. Were people in the Old Testament saved, and if so, what was their means of salvation?
4. What is the key, from a human perspective, that opens the door to salvation?
5. When the Apostle Paul argued for "justification by faith" in Romans 4, what Old Testament character did he used as his main illustration, and why?
6. What Old Testament passage declares, "The just shall live by faith?"
7. Read Hebrews 9:15. What effect, if any, did the sacrifice of Christ have upon Old Testament saints?
8. In reference to Hebrews 11, the "faith hall of fame," what was the distinguishing characteristic about each "member" listed in the chapter? Was there anything that surprised you upon reflecting on God's revelation, and if so, what?
9. In your own words describe the word picture from Numbers 21:5–9 that Jesus alluded to in John 3:14–15 as He shared gospel truth with Nicodemus.
10. From the "Salvation Strings" section of the chapter, connect Old Testament scriptures and principles with their corresponding New Testament companions as it relates to the gospel. How and why might you use these scripture "chains" in your witness?

Chapter 4

God's Covenants with Abraham and David

It was a cold February morning when I reported for jury duty in Greeneville, Tennessee. I was called to potentially serve as a juror in Federal Circuit Court. I had mixed emotions. On one hand, I was happy to serve. On the other hand, I was thinking, "I've got places to go, things to do, people to meet." The "I'm too busy for this" part of me hoped they would call everyone and anyone but me to actually go from the jury pool to the jury stand! If you've ever been called for jury duty, you can relate to this.

There were about fifty people in a waiting room just outside the courtroom. We watched a video talking about the justice system in the United States, learned how unique, special, and important jury trials are. In the courtroom, the judge reiterated some of the same points, including these:

» The American jury trial is a constitutional right. It was included in the sixth and seventh amendments to the Bill of Rights.
» Jury trials prevent tyranny from the federal government and are part of our unique checks and balances in our democratic government.

> Jury trials provide an opportunity for citizens to participate in the process of governing. In short, the jury system provides an active voice for the people.

Although I wasn't called to sit on a jury that day, the experience was a very good civics lesson. You see, our constitutional democracy is an impressive political system. You're probably aware that the majority of our founding fathers were God-fearing people. But did you know our Constitution was patterned after a covenant, God's covenant with ancient Israel?

What is a covenant? It's a morally binding commitment between two or more parties. American democracy was set up to be a government for the people, of the people, and by the people. In summary, the Constitution is a covenant between the government and the people. Biblical covenants were agreements between God and men, the foundation of those covenants being relationship—the relationship between God and men.

The concept of covenant is important in the scriptures. The word *testament* is really another word for *covenant*, so the Bible is comprised of two parts, the Old Covenant and the New Covenant (Old Testament and New Testament respectively).

In ancient times covenants could be made between two equal parties, or between a king and a subject or subjects. The king promised certain protections, and the subject or subjects promised loyalty to the king. It's critical to note that a covenant might be conditional or unconditional.

The Old Testament (Hebrew Scriptures) is much more than a history of Israel. In one sense it's also a history of the covenants in which God revealed His character, His plans, and His purposes for mankind. Most Bible scholars recognize several major covenants in the Old Testament in which God promises to do something.

For our purposes in this book, we're only going to introduce four major covenants, all critical to understanding God's redemptive plan for man: the Abrahamic Covenant, the Mosaic Covenant, the Davidic Covenant, and the New Covenant. While we won't cover the Edenic, Adamic, or Noahic covenants in this book, I commend you to study them on your own. In this chapter we'll introduce the Abrahamic and Davidic Covenants, and in chapter 5 explore the Old Covenant, also known as the Mosaic Covenant; and the New Covenant, the spiritual "economy" we as Christians are living under today.

A Brief Interlude

Before our exploration of the covenants, I want to put forth a simple disclaimer. As we ponder God's redemptive plan for mankind, I will be approaching biblical issues regarding Israel and the church through a "dispensational" paradigm, not from a "covenant" viewpoint.

In short, here are basic distinctions between covenant and dispensational viewpoints:

1. Covenant theology states essentially that Israel and the church are the same, while a dispensational viewpoint sees Israel and the church as basically two distinct entities.
2. **Single vs. double hermeneutic:** Dispensational theology interprets the Bible uniformly with one method, the historical-grammatical method. Covenant theology employs the historical-grammatical method, but also utilizes an allegorical or spiritualizing of Old Testament passages dealing with the

future of Israel and future Kingdom of God.
3. **The Purpose of History:** Covenant theology advocates that ultimate history is strictly about God's glory through the redemption of the elect. Dispensational theology advocates that ultimate history is about God's glory through the redemption of the elect, plus God's restoring Israel to its former place of glory among the nations and establishing a thousand-year reign of Christ on earth.

If you have a different theological bent, or one that is not "dispensational" in nature, don't worry. These theological differences are not salvation issues and should in no way affect our unity as followers of Jesus Christ. These issues are non-essentials regarding both salvation and Christian unity.

If you've never been exposed to this theological paradigm, I encourage you to read prayerfully and with an open mind, seeking God's truth. If you have a different view and are settled, don't worry. Again, this is not a salvation issue nor a Christian unity issue. Some aspects of the covenants we'll explore maintain continuity no matter what your theological bent, while other aspects may create divergence. In any case, my heart's desire for unity is that of the Apostle Paul, who exhorted God's people in Ephesians 4:1–6:

> I, therefore, the prisoner of the Lord, beseech you to walk worthy of the calling with which you were called, with all lowliness and gentleness, with longsuffering, bearing with one another in love, endeavoring to keep the unity of the Spirit in the bond of peace. There is one body and one Spirit, just as you were called in one hope of your calling; one Lord, one faith, one baptism; one God and Father of all, who is above all, and through all, and in you all.

Lastly, I'll include this famous quote, often attributed to Augustine, but actually from Rupertus Meldenius, a German Lutheran theologian of the early seventeenth century: **"In essentials unity, in non-essentials liberty, in all things charity."** If you've tracked with me so far, I hope you'll appreciate my heart and disclaimer, along with this brief but important interlude.

With that said, let's first explore the wonder of God's covenant with Abraham.

The Abrahamic Covenant

As mentioned, there are two basic types of covenants: conditional and unconditional. A conditional covenant is an agreement that is binding on both parties for its fulfillment. Both parties agree to fulfill certain conditions. If either party fails to meet their responsibilities, the covenant is broken, and neither party must fulfill the expectations of the covenant. An unconditional or unilateral covenant is an agreement between two parties, but only one of the two parties must do something. Nothing is required of the other party.

The Abrahamic Covenant is an unconditional covenant, and we'll briefly cover some of the highlights. We find the covenant in Genesis 12:1–3:

> Now the Lord had said to Abram: "Get out of your country, From your family And from your father's house, To a land that I will show you. I will make you a great nation; I will bless you And make your name great; And you shall be a blessing. I will bless those who bless you, And I will curse him who curses you; And in you all the families of the earth shall be blessed."

Initially, notice the unconditional nature of the covenant, as God said, "I will," five times, without one time saying, "if you," which we'll discover when studying the conditional aspect of the Mosaic, or Old Covenant later in our survey.

In addition, the ceremony recorded in Genesis 15 indicates the unconditional nature of the covenant. When a covenant was dependent upon both parties keeping commitments, then both parties would pass between the pieces of animals. In this Genesis 15 passage, God alone moves between the halves of the animals. Abraham was in a deep sleep. God's solitary action indicates that the covenant is principally His promise, as He binds Himself to it:

- Verse 1— "After these things the word of the Lord came to Abram in a vision, saying, '"Do not be afraid, Abram. I am your shield, your exceedingly great reward.'"
- Verse 5—"Then He brought him outside and said, 'Look now toward heaven, and count the stars if you are able to number them.' And He said to him, 'So shall your descendants be.'"
- Verse 7—"Then He said to him, 'I am the Lord, who brought you out of Ur of the Chaldeans, to give you this land to inherit it.'"
- Verse 8—"And he said, 'Lord God, how shall I know that I will inherit it?'"
- Verse 9—"So He said to him, 'Bring Me a three-year-old heifer, a three-year-old female goat, a three-year-old ram, a turtledove, and a young pigeon.'"
- Verse 10—" Then he brought all these to Him and cut them in two, down the middle, and placed each piece opposite the other; but he did not cut the birds in two."
- Verse 12—" Now when the sun was going down, a deep sleep fell upon Abram; and behold, horror and great darkness fell upon him."

- » Verses 17–18. "And it came to pass, when the sun went down and it was dark, that behold, there appeared a smoking oven and a burning torch that passed between those pieces. On the same day the Lord made a covenant with Abram, saying: 'To your descendants I have given this land, from the river of Egypt to the great river, the River Euphrates.'"

Notice God's individual, national, and universal promises to Abraham:

- » **Individual Promise**—God will bless him and make his name great (Genesis 12:2).
- » **National Promise**—God will make him a great nation (Israel) (Genesis 12:2).
- » **Universal Promise**—God will bless all the families of the earth through Messiah who comes from Israel (Genesis 12:3).

Regarding the individual promise to bless Abraham and make his name great, God did just that. Later in Genesis 17:5, the Lord changed Abram's name from Abram ("high father") to Abraham ("father of a multitude"): "No longer shall your name be called Abram, but your name shall be Abraham; for I have made you a father of many nations."

How great is the name of Abraham? Well, today, roughly four thousand years after his death, Abraham is revered among the three great monotheistic religions in the world—Christianity, Judaism, and Islam.

Regarding the promise to make Abraham a great nation, which was the nation of Israel, this is the most complex aspect of the covenant. While Abraham was promised a land for his nation, specifically the land of Canaan (Genesis 12:1, 7; 15:18–21; 17:8), he never lived to see the ultimate fulfillment of that promise. Remember, the land that was promised was not given to Abram, but rather to his descendants.

Centuries after Abraham died, the children of Israel took possession of the land under Joshua's leadership (Joshua 21:43). However, at no point throughout history has Israel controlled all the land God had specified would be theirs. Therefore, there remains a final fulfillment of the Abrahamic Covenant when Israel fully occupies their God-given homeland. The fulfillment will be more than a matter of geography; it will also be a season of holiness and restoration (see Ezekiel 20:40–44; 36:1–37:28), as we'll see later when we explore the New Covenant promises God made to the Jewish people and the millennial reign of Christ later in this chapter.

The land of Canaan was to become the land of Israel. While Joshua and the people of Israel did enter the promised land, God would later remove them because of their disobedience. In His faithfulness, God would also bring them back into the land of their origin, as witnessed by the birth of the modern state of Israel in 1948. Even so, the modern state of Israel is not the ultimate fulfillment of the land promise, but only a partial fulfillment. Charles L. Feinberg estimates that the original land promise found in Genesis 15 called "for a stretch of land three hundred thousand miles square miles or twelve and one-half times the size of Great Britain and Ireland."[6] This contrasts strongly with the borders of the modern state of

---

6. *Israel, the Land and the People*; H. Wayne House, general editor; pg. 24, quoting Charles L. Feinberg, *Israel: At the Center of History and Revelation*, 3rd ed. Portland: Multnomah 1980, pg. 168.

Israel, with an area of about ten thousand square miles."[7] In short, at the Second Coming of the Messiah, the fulness of this aspect of the Abrahamic Covenant will come to fruition during the millennial kingdom—the thousand-year rule and reign of Jesus, the Prince of Peace and King of Kings!

Ultimately "the land of Israel is the place where the people of God will enjoy the presence of God under the reign of God in the kingdom of God."[8] As the land of Israel is the geographical center of earth's continents, it is also the focal point of His redemptive plan for mankind, and it's the place of the outworking of His eternal purposes.

Lastly, regarding the universal promise to bless all the families of the earth, we understand that through the nation of Israel came forth Messiah Jesus, who has called and continues to call out a people from every tribe, tongue, nation, and land (Revelation 7:9). God's salvation found in Jesus Christ and the gospel message has stretched to the four corners of the earth. Hallelujah!

The Davidic Covenant

The Davidic Covenant, which is unconditional in nature, refers to God's promises to David through Nathan, the prophet. The connection of this covenant to Jesus, as we'll soon uncover, is powerful. The King of Kings will one day sit on the Davidic throne, an eternal throne!

Our starting point is 2 Samuel 7:8–17:

---

7. Ibid., pg. 24, quoting Hanan Sher, et al; *Facts about Israel*; Jerusalem: The Ministry of Foreign affairs, 1979.
8. Ibid., Ronald B. Allen; pg. 28.

Now therefore, thus shall you say to My servant David, "Thus says the Lord of hosts: 'I took you from the sheepfold, from following the sheep, to be ruler over My people, over Israel. And I have been with you wherever you have gone, and have cut off all your enemies from before you, and have made you a great name, like the name of the great men who are on the earth. Moreover I will appoint a place for My people Israel, and will plant them, that they may dwell in a place of their own and move no more; nor shall the sons of wickedness oppress them anymore, as previously, since the time that I commanded judges to be over My people Israel, and have caused you to rest from all your enemies. Also the Lord tells you that He will make you a house. "When your days are fulfilled and you rest with your fathers, I will set up your seed after you, who will come from your body, and I will establish his kingdom. He shall build a house for My name, and I will establish the throne of his kingdom forever. I will be his Father, and he shall be My son. If he commits iniquity, I will chasten him with the rod of men and with the blows of the sons of men. But My mercy shall not depart from him, as I took it from Saul, whom I removed from before you. And your house and your kingdom shall be established forever before you. Your throne shall be established forever.""" According to all these words and according to all this vision, so Nathan spoke to David.

The two unconditional promises God made are that He would make David's name great (2 Samuel 7:9) and that He would continue David's line and establish his throne to be eternal (2 Samuel 12–16).

Three key concepts from the Davidic Covenant we want to keep in mind are:

1. **It's an unconditional covenant.** Second Samuel 7:14–15 states,

"I will be his Father, and he shall be My son. If he commits iniquity, I will chasten him with the rod of men and with the blows of the sons of men. But My mercy shall not depart from him, as I took it from Saul, whom I removed from before you." Even though Solomon and his progeny might fail, note God promised that His "mercy shall not depart from Him."

2. **David's throne is eternal.** God declared in 2 Samuel 7:16, "And your house and your kingdom shall be established forever before you. Your throne shall be established forever." This covenant is later summarized in 1 Chronicles 17:11–14 and 2 Chronicles 6:16:

And it shall be, when your days are fulfilled, when you must go to be with your fathers, that I will set up your seed after you, who will be of your sons; and I will establish his kingdom. He shall build Me a house, and I will establish his throne forever. I will be his Father, and he shall be My son; and I will not take My mercy away from him, as I took it from him who was before you. And I will establish him in My house and in My kingdom forever; and his throne shall be established forever."'"

—1 Chronicles 17:11–14

Therefore, Lord God of Israel, now keep what You promised Your servant David my father, saying, "You shall not fail to have a man sit before Me on the throne of Israel, only if your sons take heed to their way, that they walk in My law as you have walked before Me."

—2 Chronicles 6:16

3. **The Abrahamic land promise is reaffirmed.** God reaffirms the promise of the land that He made with Israel in the Abrahamic Covenant. This promise is seen in 2 Samuel 7:10, "...

I will appoint a place for My people Israel, and will plant them, that they may dwell in a place of their own and move no more; nor shall the sons of wickedness oppress them anymore, as previously."

In Isaiah 9:6–7, a powerful messianic prophecy, we find the ultimate fulfillment of the Davidic Covenant:

> For unto us a Child is born, Unto us a Son is given; And the government will be upon His shoulder. And His name will be called Wonderful, Counselor, Mighty God, Everlasting Father, Prince of Peace. Of the increase of His government and peace There will be no end, Upon the throne of David and over His kingdom, To order it and establish it with judgment and justice From that time forward, even forever. The zeal of the Lord of hosts will perform this.

When Jesus returns to this earth as King of Kings and Lord of Lords, He will sit on the throne of David, the eternal throne of God, forever. Hallelujah!

Putting It All Together

At this point in our survey, I want to introduce the important future reality called the millennial reign of Christ, also called the "Millennium." The Millennium is important because both the Abrahamic and Davidic covenants, along with the New Covenant, which we'll address in Chapter 5, are fulfilled during this era in God's redemptive history.

The Millennium (also known as the Millennial Kingdom) is the thousand-year reign of Jesus on the Earth, that occurs after the

Tribulation and before all the people of the world are sent to either heaven or hell. While some Bible scholars seek to interpret the thousand years in an allegorical manner, the author holds to a literal interpretation of the many passages speaking of this time. For example, six times in Revelation 20:2–7 the Millennial Kingdom is specifically said to be one thousand years in length:

> He laid hold of the dragon, that serpent of old, who is the Devil and Satan, and bound him for a thousand years; and he cast him into the bottomless pit, and shut him up, and set a seal on him, so that he should deceive the nations no more till **the thousand years** were finished. But after these things he must be released for a little while. And I saw thrones, and they sat on them, and judgment was committed to them. Then I saw the souls of those who had been beheaded for their witness to Jesus and for the word of God, who had not worshiped the beast or his image, and had not received his mark on their foreheads or on their hands. And they lived and reigned with Christ for **a thousand years.** But the rest of the dead did not live again until **the thousand years** were finished. This is the first resurrection. Blessed and holy is he who has part in the first resurrection. Over such the second death has no power, but they shall be priests of God and of Christ, and shall reign with Him **a thousand years.** Now when **the thousand years** have expired, Satan will be released from his prison.

If God wished to communicate "a long period of time," He could have simply done so without explicitly and repeatedly mentioning an exact time frame.

During the Millennium, Jesus will reign as King over Israel and all the nations of the world:

> Now it shall come to pass in the latter days That the mountain of the Lord's house Shall be established on the top of the mountains, And shall be exalted above the hills; And all nations shall flow to it. Many people shall come and say, "Come, and let us go up to the mountain of the Lord, To the house of the God of Jacob; He will teach us His ways, And we shall walk in His paths." For out of Zion shall go forth the law, And the word of the Lord from Jerusalem. He shall judge between the nations, And rebuke many people; They shall beat their swords into plowshares, And their spears into pruning hooks; Nation shall not lift up sword against nation, Neither shall they learn war anymore.
>
> —Isaiah 2:2–4

> Behold! My Servant whom I uphold,
> My Elect One in whom My soul delights!
> I have put My Spirit upon Him;
> He will bring forth justice to the Gentiles.
>
> —Isaiah 42:1

During the Millennium, the world will live in peace:

> The wolf also shall dwell with the lamb, The leopard shall lie down with the young goat, The calf and the young lion and the fatling together; And a little child shall lead them. The cow and the bear shall graze; Their young ones shall lie down together; And the lion shall eat straw like the ox. The nursing child shall play by the cobra's hole, And the weaned child shall put his hand in the viper's den. They shall not hurt nor destroy in all My holy mountain, For the earth shall be full of the knowledge of the Lord As the waters

cover the sea.

—Isaiah 11:6–9

My people will dwell in a peaceful habitation, In secure dwellings, and in quiet resting places.

—Isaiah 32:18

The purpose of the thousand-year reign is to fulfill promises God made to the world that cannot be fulfilled while Satan is free and humans have political authority. Some of God's promises were given specifically to Israel (Abrahamic and Davidic covenants). Others were given to Jesus, the nations of the world, and creation. All of these will be fulfilled during Jesus' thousand-year reign. The fulfillment of these covenants and other promises of God rests on a literal, physical, future kingdom.

As we've explored the remarkable promises of God found in the Abrahamic and Davidic covenants, we praise and thank Him, who is faithful. Yes, our God is a covenant-keeping God. **"For all the promises of God in Him are Yes, and in Him Amen, to the glory of God through us"** (2 Corinthians 1:20).

Chapter 4 Study Guide

1. What is a covenant? What is a biblical covenant?
2. What two types of biblical covenants exist and why is the distinction important?
3. What are the basic differences between "dispensational" and "covenant" theologies as presented? Do or should these matters affect a person's salvation or people's Christian unity?
4. Is the Abrahamic Covenant conditional or unconditional? What are the three promises God made to Abraham in Genesis 12:1–3?
5. Describe how God has kept those promises to Abraham. Have they all been completely fulfilled? Discuss.
6. Was the Davidic Covenant conditional or unconditional? What promises did God make to David in 2 Samuel 7?
7. According to 2 Samuel 7:16, what is the nature of David's throne, and why is that important?
8. How does Isaiah 9:6–7 relate to the Davidic Covenant?
9. Unpack Isaiah 9:6–7, listing as many descriptors and characteristics about the Messiah as you're able.
10. What is the millennial reign of Christ and why is it important?

Chapter 5

The Old Covenant Versus the New Covenant

Every world-class guitarist began just as any other human being—striving to pluck strings and make sweet-sounding music—as a beginner. In fact, the common starting point for every musician must be to have an instrument, the essential in making music.

Our daughter, Shoshi, is a good ukulele player. When she began playing, we purchased a "beginner uke." It was an instrument that would satisfy a beginner's needs. It stayed in tune and was of sufficient quality. It met her needs at that particular time. As she learned, progressed, and began playing all the time, she desired something more from the instrument. A higher quality ukulele would bring forth a more refined sound and, in essence, make our daughter sound better. The highest priced ukuleles cost in the thousands of dollars. However, one doesn't need to spend that kind of money for a high quality "uke" that makes a more refined sound. Today, Shoshi has several ukuleles, and she's happy with their quality and sound.

While "better" is a requisite in matching accomplished musicians with higher quality instruments, "better" is also the operative word for our continued study of covenants as we compare and contrast the Old Covenant with the New Covenant.

The Old Covenant, also known as the Mosaic Covenant, originated at Mt. Sinai with God birthing the nation of Israel and giving them the law. The New Covenant, originally given to Israel and Judah in Jeremiah, was instituted by Jesus at the last supper in Matthew 26:28, when He declared, "For this is My blood of the new covenant, which is shed for many for the remission of sins."

In this chapter, we'll explore these covenants and learn why the New Covenant is better than the Old Covenant, and why it matters for the Christian today.

The Old Covenant

The Old Covenant, also known as the Mosaic Covenant, is a conditional covenant made between God and the nation of Israel at Mount Sinai. I would encourage you to do a study of Exodus 19–24, which details the covenant. For our purposes, we're only going to touch some high points.

While sometimes referred to as the Sinai Covenant, it's more often called the Mosaic Covenant since Moses was God's chosen leader of Israel at that time. Our starting point of introduction is Exodus 19:4–8:

> "'You have seen what I did to the Egyptians, and how I bore you on eagles' wings and brought you to Myself. Now therefore, if you will indeed obey My voice and keep My covenant, then you shall be a special treasure to Me above all people; for all the earth is Mine. And you shall be to Me a kingdom of priests and a holy nation.' These are the words which you shall speak to the children of Israel." So Moses came and called for the elders of the people, and laid before them all these words which the LORD commanded

him. Then all the people answered together and said, "All that the LORD has spoken we will do." So Moses brought back the words of the people to the LORD.

In verse 4, we find God reminding Israel that He is their Savior, the One who snatched them from their oppressors. In verse 5, He promised to make them His "special treasure" if they entered into the covenant with Him. The Lord declared Israel will be a "kingdom of priests" and a "holy nation" in verse 6. At this moment in God's redemptive plan, Israel was called to be His representatives to the nations, the gentiles.

The conditional nature of the Mosaic Covenant is important here, as it came with an "if." If Israel acted in obedience to the covenant, they would be blessed; if they disobeyed, they would be cursed. Deuteronomy 28 lays out blessings and curses for obedience and disobedience:

> Now it shall come to pass, if you diligently obey the voice of the LORD your God, to observe carefully all His commandments which I command you today, that the LORD your God will set you high above all nations of the earth. And all these blessings shall come upon you and overtake you, because you obey the voice of the LORD your God. ... But it shall come to pass, if you do not obey the voice of the LORD your God, to observe carefully all His commandments and His statutes which I command you today, that all these curses will come upon you and overtake you.
>
> —Deuteronomy 28:1–2, 15

Some of the other blessings were provision of agricultural fruitfulness and protection from enemies (Deuteronomy 28:7–8). Curses or judgments upon disobedience included disease, drought, defeat by enemies, and ultimate deportation (Deuteronomy 28:16–37).

Any cursory study of the Jewish scriptures, or Old Testament, reveals that Israel failed to uphold their end of the covenant. In short, they broke that covenant, yet God, in His mercy and grace, had a purpose for the Old Covenant and had a plan for another covenant, a New Covenant, which simply would be better!

Critical Pieces of the Old Covenant Puzzle

Remember, we've noted that in one sense the Old Testament is the New Testament concealed, and the New Testament is the Old Testament revealed. This concept comes to the fore as we compare pieces of the Old Covenant with New Covenant truth.

God's redemptive plan has always been about mankind, not Jews or gentiles exclusively. Psalm 117 illustrates the seal of redemptive truth: "Praise the Lord, all you Gentiles! Laud Him, all you peoples! For His merciful kindness is great toward us, And the truth of the Lord endures forever. Praise the Lord!"

As one Bible commentator eloquently noted, "That God looked redemptively beyond the borders of the Old Testament is made clear here in Psalm 117. The psalm looks back to God's intent for Adam and Eve in Eden and looks ahead to the ultimate fulfillment in the new heavens and earth (Revelation 21, 22)."[9]

God's redemptive plan is always for mankind. "For God so loved the world …" (John 3:16).

Although the Mosaic Covenant was holy, righteous, and good (Romans 7:12), it didn't save. God didn't design the Mosaic law as a means of salvation. Rather the Mosaic Covenant was an affirmation

---

9. *MacArthur Study Bible*, pg. 848

of the relationship God had with His chosen people Israel in order to accomplish His purposes for mankind. Forgiveness has always been obtained through faith, as we've noted earlier (Genesis 15:6; Micah 6:6–8; Romans 4:1–5:2; and Romans 7:13–25). The Mosaic law showed Israel their sin and need for salvation. In fact, the law is a tutor to lead people to the Messiah! Galatians 3:24 states, "Therefore the law was our tutor to bring us to Christ, that we might be justified by faith."

The Mosaic or Old Covenant accomplished its purposes for that particular era of redemptive history, just as a beginner's instrument serves its purpose for the individual who is just starting their musical journey. Yet there was something more to come, something better in God's economy, that would supplant and replace the Old Covenant. It was the New Covenant.

New Covenant Promises

As Christians we live under the New Covenant economy. Interestingly, it was a promise initially given to the Jewish people. Our starting point is Jeremiah 31:31–34, where God announced this New Covenant promise:

> Behold, the days are coming, says the Lord, when I will make a new covenant with the house of Israel and with the house of Judah—not according to the covenant that I made with their fathers in the day that I took them by the hand to lead them out of the land of Egypt, My covenant which they broke, though I was a husband to them, says the Lord. But this is the covenant that I will make with the house of Israel after those days, says the Lord: I will put My law in their minds, and write it on their hearts; and I will be their

God, and they shall be My people. No more shall every man teach his neighbor, and every man his brother, saying, "Know the Lord," for they all shall know Me, from the least of them to the greatest of them, says the Lord. For I will forgive their iniquity, and their sin I will remember no more.

Jeremiah shared a prophecy with the Jewish people about the future. This was first and foremost a covenant God made with the Jewish people. When Jeremiah penned this prophecy, the northern kingdom of Israel had already been taken captive by the Assyrians about a century earlier in 722 B.C., while the southern kingdom of Judah would soon be judged for their rebelliousness against God, falling to Babylon in 586 B.C.

Jeremiah provided the Jewish people a future hope in the midst of their pain. So, we have this declaration given to Jeremiah from God. Interestingly, the majority of the remaining information about the New Covenant is found in the New Testament.

First, note the reason for the New Covenant in verses 31–32. God had to make another covenant with the Jewish people because they broke the first covenant, the Old Covenant. We see the reason for the New Covenant. Notice its characteristics.

In verses 33–34, following the pain of judgement, comes the hope of promise.

> But this is the covenant that I will make with the house of Israel after those days, says the Lord: I will put My law in their minds, and write it on their hearts; and I will be their God, and they shall be My people. No more shall every man teach his neighbor, and every man his brother, saying, "Know the Lord," for they all shall know Me, from the least of them to the greatest of them, says the

Lord. For I will forgive their iniquity, and their sin I will remember no more.

This is a future time when God will write His law on their hearts, they will all know the Lord, and they will all be forgiven. The Jewish prophet Ezekiel explained in detail this future reality which will occur at the Second Coming of Jesus, when the Jewish people see Jesus, whom they've pierced, and mourn. God's response will be to give them a spirit of grace and supplication, and they will believe and will be saved.

Note the similarity to New Testament concepts like cleansing from sin, the new birth, and the gift of the Holy Spirit we find in Ezekiel 36, as part of the future New Covenant fulfillment:

> For I will take you from among the nations, gather you out of all countries, and bring you into your own land. Then I will sprinkle clean water on you, and you shall be clean; I will cleanse you from all your filthiness and from all your idols. I will give you a new heart and put a new spirit within you; I will take the heart of stone out of your flesh and give you a heart of flesh. I will put My Spirit within you and cause you to walk in My statutes, and you will keep My judgments and do them. Then you shall dwell in the land that I gave to your fathers; you shall be My people, and I will be your God.
>
> —Ezekiel 36:24–28

As Christians, we can certainly relate to those same promises of God. The Lord has cleansed us of all sin through the shed blood of the Messiah. He's written His law on our hearts, and He's given us a new heart and a new Spirit—all under the New Covenant. We must ask, "How does that covenant, originally promised to the Jewish people in Jeremiah's time and ultimately fulfilled during the Second Coming of Jesus, apply to the Christian today?"

Matthew 26:27 provides the answer. While Jesus was celebrating the Passover meal at the last supper, He lifted the third cup, the cup of redemption and uttered these words: "Then He took the cup, and gave thanks, and gave it to them, saying, 'Drink from it, all of you. For this is My blood of the new covenant, which is shed for many for the remission of sins'" (Matthew 26:27–28).

The blood of what covenant, shed for many for the forgiveness of sins? The New Covenant. Look at Hebrews 9:15: "And for this reason He [Jesus] is the Mediator of the new covenant, by means of death, for the redemption of the transgressions under the first covenant, that those who are called may receive the promise of the eternal inheritance."

A mediator is a go-between, so Jesus brokered this new covenant relationship between God and man. In fact, His shed blood was applied retroactively, meaning it also covered the sins of those who believed in God through the Mosaic or Old Covenant, as we discovered earlier in our study. We are all saved by grace through faith. The difference is that Old Testament saints were saved by grace through faith in God's promise of the Messiah, while as Christians we're saved by grace through faith in the provision of Messiah.

Under the New Covenant promise, believers in Messiah Jesus, whether Jew or gentile, are one together in Him, as the Apostle Paul stated in Ephesians 2:14–15, "For He Himself is our peace, who has made both one, and has broken down the middle wall of separation, having abolished in His flesh the enmity, that is, the law of commandments contained in ordinances, so as to create in Himself one new man from the two, thus making peace."

So the New Covenant promise is partially fulfilled at Jesus' first coming! The ultimate fulfillment of the New Covenant promise to the Jewish people will occur at His Second Coming. Notice the contrast between a promise partially fulfilled and a promise completely fulfilled.

I once took our son Elijah to see a Christian concert. I paid the promoter money and got the tickets. The tickets represented the promise partially fulfilled, but it was only when we showed up at the concert hall the night of the concert, showed our tickets, and took our seats, that the promise was completely fulfilled.

As Kingdom citizens under the New Covenant reality, we only experience a partial fulfillment today of God's salvation. For example, when we trust in Jesus, we're delivered from the penalty of sin. As we live our Christian lives, we are continually delivered from the power of sin. But only when we die and go to heaven or Jesus returns and brings us home, will we be delivered from the presence of sin! Additionally, we read about the promise of heaven in the New Covenant scriptures. Someday soon—maybe tomorrow—we'll enter that reality, a place with no more death, or mourning, or crying, or pain (Revelation 21:4).

The New Covenant promises are tremendous, and so are the New Covenant privileges.

New Covenant Privileges

In Acts 2 when the church was born at Pentecost, which is the Jewish Feast of Shavuot, the Holy Spirit came and filled every believer. As an aside, in a later chapter we'll explore the Trinity in the Old Testament, including the Holy Spirit. Under the Mosaic Covenant, the Spirit only filled certain people at certain times to accomplish specific purposes of God. In the Old Testament, the Spirit filled prophets, priests, and kings. For example, in Psalm 51:11, King David cried out to God not to take the Spirit from him. The Spirit's indwelling of all believers today is a huge privilege under the New Covenant.

"Now hope does not disappoint, because the love of God has been poured out in our hearts by the Holy Spirit who was given to us" (Romans 5:5). The Apostle Paul elaborated on the indwelling of the Spirit for all believers, both Jew and gentile, in Ephesians 2:17–18: "And He came and preached peace to you who were afar off and to those who were near. For through Him we both have access by one Spirit to the Father."

What are some of the other benefits of the Spirit? Well, the Holy Spirit cleanses, sanctifies, and justifies us. The Spirit intercedes for believers before the Father. The Spirit leads us into truth. The Holy Spirit comforts us in times of affliction and hardship, and the Holy Spirit refreshes us daily with hope and love.

Another privilege is that gentiles are grafted into this New Covenant promise. In Romans 11, which we'll study at length in Chapter 6, the Apostle Paul compared Israel to the natural branches of a cultivated olive tree, and the gentile believers to the branches of a wild olive tree. The natural branches (Israel) were broken off, and the wild branches (gentiles) were grafted in (Hebrews 11:11–24). Gentiles therefore have been made partakers of the New Covenant promise and inherit the blessings of redemption. You see, God's salvation doesn't exclude gentiles, nor is it exclusively for Jews. The only requirement to enter the New Covenant with God is simply to trust in Jesus. As one theologian rightly quipped, "Forgiveness has no favorites."

Finally, under the New Covenant, if anyone is in Christ, he is a new creation with new hopes and desires. Our desire to love God and others has nothing to do with old rules written in stone, but rather the law written on our hearts. The Apostle Paul explained in 2 Corinthians 3:2–3: "You are our epistle written in our hearts, known and read by all men; clearly you are an epistle of Christ, ministered by us, written not with ink but by the Spirit of the living God, not on tablets of stone but on tablets of flesh, that is, of the heart."

What is the law written on our hearts? Simply, it is not a set of rules, but a person. It's not a "what," but a "who." The law written on our hearts is none other than the Holy Spirit, which the Bible also calls the Spirit of Christ and the Spirit of life: "For the law of the Spirit of life in Christ Jesus has made me free from the law of sin and death" (Romans 8:2).

Although the law under the Old Covenant was holy, righteous, and good, it couldn't save. It simply showed the people that they were lawbreakers, sinners in need of a savior. The Mosaic law was external, and the people were limited in their ability to observe it, because the Spirit was not accessible universally for believers as it is under the New Covenant! Because we have the law written on our hearts, we now have the power now to love God and love others.

New Covenant Responsibility

We find the centerpiece of New Covenant responsibility in Matthew 28:18–20, commonly known to the believer as the great commission:

> And Jesus came and spoke to them, saying, "All authority has been given to Me in heaven and on earth. Go therefore and make disciples of all the nations, baptizing them in the name of the Father and of the Son and of the Holy Spirit, teaching them to observe all things that I have commanded you; and lo, I am with you always, even to the end of the age." Amen.

What does it mean to go and make disciples? A disciple is a follower, so making a disciple is twofold: it includes sharing our faith with those who've not yet entered that New Covenant relationship through personal faith in Jesus, as well as helping people grow in that relationship with the Lord.

So, evangelism and being witnesses for the Lord are important, but the method of our mission as New Covenant believers is different than it was for the Israelites under the Mosaic Covenant. Ancient Israel was called to be a kingdom of priests to the nations, a light to the gentiles. The way they accomplished that mission was to bring converts, or proselytes, into the community of faith. God told them not to go out into the nations, lest they fall into idolatry. Under the New Covenant, we as God's people are called to go out to all nations, bringing the glory of God and the truth of God with us.

Making disciples also means to support other believers' walk with God. In John 13:34, Jesus said, "A new commandment I give to you, that you love one another; as I have loved you, that you also love one another." There are lots of "one anothers" in the New Testament—fifty-nine to be precise. Among them, we're called to serve, pray, instruct, forgive, confess sins, carry each others burdens, and submit to one another. Jesus said: "To whom much is given, much is expected."

New Covenant Fulfillment

Remember, New Covenant promises were originally made to Israel and Judah in Jeremiah 31. Although Israel is back in the land, God has not yet written His law on their hearts, and He has not forgiven their sins. This will occur at the Second Coming of Christ when the

Lord establishes His Kingdom on Earth during the Millennium (Zechariah 12:10–13:9; Hosea 2:19–23).

> For I will take you from among the nations, gather you out of all countries, and bring you into your own land. Then I will sprinkle clean water on you, and you shall be clean; I will cleanse you from all your filthiness and from all your idols. I will give you a new heart and put a new spirit within you; I will take the heart of stone out of your flesh and give you a heart of flesh. I will put My Spirit within you and cause you to walk in My statutes, and you will keep My judgments and do them. Then you shall dwell in the land that I gave to your fathers; you shall be My people, and I will be your God. I will deliver you from all your uncleannesses. I will call for the grain and multiply it, and bring no famine upon you. And I will multiply the fruit of your trees and the increase of your fields, so that you need never again bear the reproach of famine among the nations. Then you will remember your evil ways and your deeds that were not good; and you will loathe yourselves in your own sight, for your iniquities and your abominations.
>
> —Ezekiel 36:24–31

And I will pour on the house of David and on the inhabitants of Jerusalem the Spirit of grace and supplication; then they will look on Me whom they pierced. Yes, they will mourn for Him as one mourns for his only son, and grieve for Him as one grieves for a firstborn.

—Zechariah 12:10

Better, Better, Better

When comparing the Old Covenant with the New Covenant, a simple yet profound understanding is found in the concept of "better"—a better covenant established on better promises which includes a better sacrifice and better priesthood, as the book of Hebrews declares.

> But now He has obtained a more excellent ministry, inasmuch as He is also Mediator of a better covenant, which was established on better promises. For if that first covenant had been faultless, then no place would have been sought for a second. Because finding fault with them, He says: "Behold, the days are coming, says the Lord, when I will make a new covenant with the house of Israel and with the house of Judah—" ... In that He says, "A new covenant," He has made the first obsolete. Now what is becoming obsolete and growing old is ready to vanish away.
>
> —Hebrews 8:6-8, 13

> But Christ came as High Priest of the good things to come, with the greater and more perfect tabernacle not made with hands, that is, not of this creation. Not with the blood of goats and calves, but with His own blood He entered the Most Holy Place once for all, having obtained eternal redemption.
>
> —Hebrews 9:11–12

> And every priest stands ministering daily and offering repeatedly the same sacrifices, which can never take away sins. But this Man, after He had offered one sacrifice for sins forever, sat down at the right hand of God, from that time waiting till His enemies are made His footstool. For by one offering He has perfected forever those who are being sanctified.
>
> —Hebrews 10:11–14

As we ponder the wonder of all our New Covenant blessings in

Messiah Jesus, may we praise God for them and echo in our hearts the words of the psalmist, who in Psalm 103 exclaimed,

> Bless the Lord, O my soul; And all that is within me, bless His holy name! Bless the Lord, O my soul, And forget not all His benefits: Who forgives all your iniquities, Who heals all your diseases, Who redeems your life from destruction, Who crowns you with loving-kindness and tender mercies, Who satisfies your mouth with good things, So that your youth is renewed like the eagle's.
>
> —Psalm 103:1–5

Chapter 5 Study Guide

1. Was the Old Covenant conditional or unconditional?
2. What were the basic conditions of the Old Covenant?
3. According to the Apostle Paul in Romans 7:12, what were the characteristics of the Old Covenant law? Also, according to Paul in Galatians 3:24, how would the "law" aid people as it related to the Messiah?
4. Was adherence to the Old Covenant a means of salvation? What would disobedience to the Old Covenant law reveal to the Jewish people?
5. Where is the New Covenant promise originally declared by God in the Jewish Bible, and who were the original recipients of the promise?
6. According to Jeremiah 31:31–34, what were the main characteristics of the New Covenant?
7. Where in the New Testament record did Jesus declare the New Covenant promise accessible for all people, anyone who trusts in Him?
8. According to the Apostle Paul in Ephesians 2:14–15, what is the relationship between Jews and gentiles who know the Lord Jesus?
9. What are some New Covenant privileges? What are some New Covenant responsibilities?
10. When will the ultimate fulfillment of the New Covenant promise made to Israel and Judah in Jeremiah 31 occur?

Chapter 6

Israel in Romans 9–11

I was a professional tennis coach for fourteen years. After playing the junior circuit in Florida as a youth, competing at the collegiate level for one year, and graduating from college, I began coaching full time. I loved it. Although I don't coach tennis anymore, I'm still a sports enthusiast!

Through my years of teaching tennis, I discovered a common mistake many recreational players make is to hold the racquet too tightly. Their incorrect assumption is that if they hold the racquet tighter, they will be able to hit the tennis ball harder. It is not so. In fact, the "less is more" principle applies here. I have taught countless players the proper way to hold the tennis racquet. Without getting too technical, it's more of a feel with the fingers applying pressure on the grip of the racquet, rather than the palm of the hand exerting pressure on the grip. Being able to hold the tennis racquet properly will enable an individual to hit the ball with maximum effectiveness and efficiency.

Interestingly, the "less is more" principle applies to other sports, not just tennis. In similar fashion, the "death grip" doesn't work with a baseball or softball bat, nor does it help the golfer hit the golf ball farther.

You might find it intriguing to know that the "less is more" principle may be applied to salvation. You may be thinking, "How does that work? Pray tell!" Just as "less is more" is applied to different sports skills, God's principles for salvation apply not only in an individual sense, but also in a corporate sense. You see, just as individuals are saved by grace, so the nation of Israel will be saved by grace. Just as individual people are saved by grace through the imputed righteousness of the Messiah applied by faith, so it will be for the nation of Israel in the future, as we'll discover in this chapter.

There's more. As we embark on a brief journey through Romans 9–11, we'll uncover many salvation principles for individuals that were taught in Romans 1–8 and are now applied to corporate Israel in this powerful section of the Holy Scriptures.

Big Picture Themes from Romans

When we think of salvation doctrine in the New Testament, the book of Romans is a landmark work. Under the inspiration of the Holy Spirit, the Apostle Paul masterfully unpacked salvation theology and the outflowing of that truth in application to Christian living. Paul demonstrated that in the cross of Christ, God judges sin and at the same time shows his saving mercy.

Some of the key themes in Romans include:

» The Mosaic law is good and holy, but only Christ can remove sin and overcome its power (2:12–29; 3:9–20; 5:20; 7:1–25; 9:30–10:8).
» Through the righteousness of God, sin is judged and salvation is provided (3:21–26; 5:12–19; 6:1–10; 7:1–6; 8:1–4).
» With the coming of Messiah Jesus, a new age of redemptive history has begun (1:1–7; 3:21–26; 5:1–8:39).
» The atoning death of Jesus Christ is central to God's plan of sal-

vation (3:21–26; 4:23–25; 5:6–11, 15–19; 6:1–10; 7:4–6; 8:1–4).
- » Justification is by faith alone (1:16–4:25; 9:30–10:21).
- » Those who are in Christ Jesus have a sure hope of future glory (5:1–8:39).
- » By the power of the Holy Spirit, those who have died with Christ live a new life (2:25–29; 6:1–7:6; 8:1–39).
- » Because of God's grace, Christians should be morally pure, should show love to their neighbors, should be good citizens, and should welcome their fellow believers into fullest fellowship (12:1–15:7).

In this chapter these two themes from Romans will be in focus:

- » **God is sovereign in salvation.** He works all things according to his plan (9:1–11:36).
- » **God fulfills his promises to both Jews and gentiles** (1:18–4:25; 9:1–11:36; 14:1–15:13).

Introducing Romans 9–11

A simple outline of Romans can be to simply divide the book into three parts:

1. individual salvation (Romans 1–8);
2. corporate salvation of Israel (Romans 9–11); and
3. the outworking of salvation (Romans 12–16).

As we journey on redemption road and reflect on God's redemptive plan for mankind, we stop for a moment on our journey at Romans 9–11.

To some people, this section of Scripture is oddly placed. Why? In Romans 1–8, Paul elaborated on the salvation by God's grace obtained through faith in the righteousness of God in Christ. In Romans 12–16, he unpacked the application of our faith, where he provided instruction for the believer in turning our theology into biology, living out our faith. But what of Romans 9–11, where Israel is the focus?

This is the focus of our brief study of this section of Romans. As we'll discover, sovereignty in salvation is not only applied to the individual, but is also applied to His chosen people, Israel.

We'll find that God has a purpose in Israel's corporate rejection of Messiah Jesus at His first coming. In fact, to the surprise of some, the Word of God will reveal that Israel's rejection of the Messiah is neither complete, permanent, nor final. Rather, God is not done with Israel. He has a plan, a marvelous plan, for the future of His people. As Romans 11:26 declares, "… so all Israel will be saved. …"

The basic outline for Romans 9–11 is as follows:

- » Romans 9: God's past dealings with Israel—Israel's chosen election.
- » Romans 10: God's present dealings with Israel—The remnant is saved by grace, the rest are blinded by works.
- » Romans 11: God's purpose and plan for Israel's future

For our purposes we'll spend the most time on Romans 11, where we'll see the panorama of redemption applied wonderfully to Israel! We'll briefly introduce Romans 9–10, while spending more time on Romans 11.

The study of Romans 9–11 is critical in light of the entire letter. Up to this point, the Apostle Paul has keenly argued that a person has a right standing before God by simply trusting God's work through Messiah Jesus' sacrifice on the cross. As God's covenant nation, why has Israel rejected God's Messiah, while many gentiles have accepted this same Messiah for salvation?

Paul dealt with this issue in Romans 9. After he expressed deep grief over Israel's rejection of God (vv.1–5), Paul demonstrated that God's salvation is not inconsistent with His promises (vv.6–13). In Romans 9:6–13, Paul argued that though all are Abraham's children, not all are Abraham's seed—only those who are called. While Ishmael and Esau were children and grandchildren of Abraham, so were Isaac and Jacob, yet only the latter two were considered seed, or the children of promises. This speaks to God's sovereignty in election.

In Romans 9:14–29, Paul asserted that the rejection of Israel by God is inconsistent with God's justice. He argued that the Lord will extend mercy and compassion on whomever He wills. Thus, the Lord will extend mercy and compassion upon some Jewish people and upon some gentiles.

In Romans 10, Paul focused on God's present dealings with Israel—the remnant is saved by grace, while the rest are blinded by works. In Romans 10:5–13, the apostle asserted that Israel had rejected Old Testament teaching of righteousness by faith, which we explored earlier in our survey. Instead, Paul argued that they attempted to attain righteousness through works. In this section he quoted various Old Testament passages, including Leviticus 18:5, Deuteronomy 30:12–14, Isaiah 28:16, and Joel 2:32.

Newsflash! The early church was exclusively Jewish prior to the conversion of Cornelius and his household in Acts 10. They were the first gentile converts in the book of Acts. Remember, the first disciples of Jesus, including Peter, James, and John, were Jewish.

Additionally, the three thousand people who were saved at Pentecost in Acts 2:41 were Jewish. This was the remnant in the first century, and God is faithful!

When Paul wrote the book of Romans in the first century, the church in Rome had a mix of Jews and gentiles. The Jewish believers were part of the remnant, while the gentile believers were part of God's salvation promises to the nations He had made through the Jewish prophets of old.

Now we come to Romans 11, the core of our study in this chapter. Romans 11 is so important because it lays out God's future purpose and plan for Israel, and it is good!

The Perception: God Cast Israel Away (Romans 11:1–10)

In verse 1, Paul dealt with this perception that even today exists among many in the church, which answers the question, "Is God finished with Israel?" He wrote, "I say then, has God cast away His people? Certainly not! ..." The reason Paul had to raise the question in the first place was that in chapters 9 and 10 he'd been writing about Israel's rejection of the gospel of Jesus, and then he had to emphatically clarify that Israel's rejection of the gospel is neither total nor final! Notice verse 2, "God has not cast away His people whom He foreknew. ..." Paul then illustrates his point in verses 2–6 by citing Elijah's perception from 1 Kings 19:

> God has not cast away His people whom He foreknew. Or do you not know what the Scripture says of Elijah, how he pleads with God against Israel, saying, "Lord, they have killed Your prophets and torn down Your altars, and I alone am left, and they seek my life"? But what does the divine response say to him? "I have

reserved for Myself seven thousand men who have not bowed the knee to Baal." Even so then, at this present time there is a remnant according to the election of grace. And if by grace, then it is no longer of works; otherwise grace is no longer grace. But if it is of works, it is no longer grace; otherwise work is no longer work.

—Romans 11:2–6

Elijah thought he was the last prophet left standing in Israel after he defeated the four hundred and fifty false prophets of Baal on Mt. Carmel. Wicked King Ahab and his corrupt wife, Jezebel, were hot on his trail, and he was discouraged and on the run. God had to set Elijah straight and tell him the truth about the situation. The truth was that God Himself had preserved a remnant of true prophets, seven thousand to be exact, according to His grace. Elijah's erroneous perception of Israel's condition in his day had to be corrected by God. Elijah was sincere, authentic, and even godly—yet he didn't get the whole picture. Only the Lord sees the beginning from the end, and just as He provided Elijah clarity in the midst of his confusion, God provides us clarity regarding His relationship with Israel. Is God finished with Israel? No!

Over the course of church history, many have identified the church as the replacement of Israel. They claim that since the Jews were responsible for the death of Jesus, God was finished with Israel, and the church has replaced her. Paul dealt with that perception. Here Paul used this example from Elijah's life to help clear up any misperceptions regarding God's dealings with Israel.

Paul continued in Romans 11:7–10:

What then? Israel has not obtained what it seeks; but the elect have obtained it, and the rest were blinded. Just as it is written: "God has given them a spirit of stupor, Eyes that they should not see

And ears that they should not hear, To this very day." And David says: "Let their table become a snare and a trap, A stumbling block and a recompense to them. Let their eyes be darkened, so that they do not see, And bow down their back always."

Paul quoted from King David and the prophet Isaiah from the Old Testament to make the point that God has given Israel what the Bible calls a state of stupor or spiritual hardening. Israel had sought to be righteous through good works, not through faith, yet God has preserved a remnant according to the election of grace, that remnant including those who were made righteous through faith in the righteous one, Messiah Jesus. The Jewish people as a nation rejected Jesus and the Jewish religious authorities categorically rejected Him in Paul's day. Still, there were still thousands of individual Jewish people who believed in Jesus as the Messiah, like Peter, James, and John, along with the rest of the disciples, as we've noted.

Though God has blinded the rest of them for a reason, we see Israel's rejection is not total. And as in the first century, we see that same spiritual dynamic in the world today. There are thousands and thousands of Jewish believers in Jesus, like me, yet Israel as a nation rejects Jesus as the Messiah. I've had believers ask me, "Larry, why don't the Jewish people get it? Why do they reject Jesus when He is their Messiah?" For the same reason the world as a whole rejects Jesus—unbelief. "He was in the world, and the world was made through Him, and the world did not know Him. He came to His own, and His own did not receive Him." (John 1:10–11).

This is God's plan, but it's not the whole story, nor is it the end of the story, and we'll find out the purpose of this plan in just a moment. Practically speaking, are you going through a trial where you feel alone and confused in an area of your life? Look for clarity in the Word of God and trust Him for guidance in your time of need, as He did for Elijah. Sometimes we feel alone, yet we're not. The Lord knows every detail of our lives, and He's always working behind the scenes. The God of Israel neither sleeps nor slumbers. In Jeremiah 29:11, God spoke these words through the prophet: "For I know the thoughts that I think toward you, says the Lord, thoughts of peace and not of evil, to give you a future and a hope." God didn't abandon Elijah. He hasn't totally rejected Israel, and He's never going to let you down either.

The Purpose of Israel's Blindness: Romans 11:11–24

After Paul dealt with the perception that God has cast away His people. he then explained the amazing purpose for Israel's blindness in verses 11–24. Verse 11 reads: "I say then, have they stumbled that they should fall? Certainly not! But through their fall, to provoke them to jealousy, salvation has come to the Gentiles." Ah! The purpose of Israel's blindness is so salvation would extend to the gentiles, or nations, of the earth, as was foretold by the prophet Isaiah. God's plan from before the foundation of the Earth was to reveal Himself to the world through the Messiah of Israel.

In Isaiah 49:6, some seven hundred years before Jesus walked this Earth as a man, God spoke through the prophet these remarkable words: "Indeed He says, 'It is too small a thing that You should be My Servant To raise up the tribes of Jacob, And to restore the preserved ones of Israel; I will also give You as a light to the Gentiles, That You should be My salvation to the ends of the earth.'" In John 8:12, Jesus referred to Himself as the Light of the world. The purpose of salvation for the gentiles is to provoke Israel to jealousy. As one Bible commentator noted, "It is similar to offering a toy to a child, who then refuses it. However, when the toy is offered to another child, the first child then wants it." Those of us who are parents can certainly relate to this.

Then in verse 12 Paul continued, "Now if their fall is riches for the world, and their failure riches for the Gentiles, how much more their fullness!" So, God's aim for the Jewish people is not their fall, but their recovery. Gentiles are saved not only for their sake but for the sake of Israel. In reality, gentile salvation is a means to an end. Praise God!

In other words, Israel's fall means salvation for the nations, and ultimately that blessing of salvation to the nations will rest upon Israel. In Romans 11:17–24, Paul warned gentiles against pride and arrogance because of Israel's rejection of the gospel. He talked about two olive trees. The wild olive tree represents gentile Christians, and the olive tree, also called the natural branches, represents national Israel. Some, but not all, of the branches of Israel were removed. Paul then explained in Romans 11:17–18 the relationship between the two: "And if some of the branches were broken off, and you, being a wild olive tree, were grafted in among them, and with them became a partaker of the root and fatness of the olive tree, do not boast against the branches. But if you do boast, remember that you do not support the root, but the root supports you." God always preserved a believing remnant of Jewish people from the olive tree, Israel.

Why would Paul use this word picture about olive trees? Well, olives were an important crop in the ancient world, and although trees often lived for hundreds of years, individual branches eventually stopped producing olives. When that happened, branches from younger trees were grafted in to restore productivity. Paul's point is that the old, unproductive branches, representing unbelieving Israel, were broken off, and branches from the wild tree, representing gentiles, were grafted in. This is the cultivated olive tree in Romans 11:24 made of Jews and gentiles. This is the church, made up of Jewish and gentile believers in Jesus. God has made one new man out of the two. You and I, whether we're Jewish or gentile, if we know Christ, are one in Him.

When Paul wrote of the wild olive tree partaking of the root and the fatness, he was simply saying gentiles are partaking in a spiritual sense the richness of God's covenant He made with Abraham. You and I, as believers in Jesus, are spiritual seeds of Abraham. I, as a Jew, am also a physical seed of Abraham.

The important thing for anyone is that they become spiritual seed of Abraham. Jesus said, "... unless one is born again, he cannot see the kingdom of God" (John 3:3). He was talking about a spiritual birth. To experience that new birth, a person must believe in Jesus. As I like to tell people on occasion, "Salvation is not about your 'Jewishness,' nor is it about your 'gentileness'—it's about your 'Jesusness.' Do you know Him?"

What Paul was saying in a sense is this: Don't be prideful because you're a gentile believer in the midst of Israel's hard heart. It's because of Israel that God has brought forth the Savior of the world, and it's the blessing of salvation to the nations that will precipitate salvation to Israel in the future.

In Romans 11:23–24 Paul referred to that time when the natural branches will be grafted back in:

> ... if they do not continue in unbelief, will be grafted in, for God is able to graft them in again. For if you were cut out of the olive tree which is wild by nature, and were grafted contrary to nature into a cultivated olive tree, how much more will these, who are natural branches, be grafted into their own olive tree?

What he was saying is that in the future, national Israel will repent of their unbelief and embrace Messiah Jesus. Certainly the misperception that God is finished with Israel over the course of church history has in part created an environment for Christian anti-Semitism to abound at various times. I need only to mention the pogroms, the Spanish Inquisition, and the Crusades to remind us that the Christian church doesn't have a great track record in dealing with Jewish people.

The Plan for Israel's Salvation: Romans 11:25–36

In the final section, Paul wrote God's glorious plan for the future salvation of Israel. In Romans 11:25–26 he joyously declared:

> For I do not desire, brethren, that you should be ignorant of this mystery, lest you should be wise in your own opinion, that blindness in part has happened to Israel until the fullness of the Gentiles has come in. And so all Israel will be saved, as it is written: "The Deliverer will come out of Zion, And He will turn away ungodliness from Jacob.

In Romans 11:25 Paul didn't want the brethren to be ignorant of this mystery. This word "mystery" in the New Testament refers to truth not previously revealed. Specifically, the mystery is that Israel's hardening is partial, and it will only last for a divinely specified time, until the fullness of the gentiles has come in. This is the completion of what we know as the Church Age, when all the gentiles from all the nations who will be saved are saved. God knows the beginning from the end.

When that time comes, Romans 11:26 exclaims that all Israel will be saved. Paul quoted from Isaiah 59 about the Deliverer coming from Zion to remove ungodliness from Jacob, which refers to Israel, and taking away their sins. Maybe you're wondering what it means that "all Israel will be saved." Some Bible commentators believe Israel in this verse refers to the whole nation. Others believe it refers to all Jewish people everywhere in the world, including the nation of Israel, who are alive when Jesus returns.

Zechariah 12:10 refers to the Second Coming of Christ, when the Jewish people repent and turn to Him. God said through the prophet, "And I will pour on the house of David and on the inhabitants of Jerusalem the Spirit of grace and supplication; then they will look on Me whom they pierced. Yes, they will mourn for Him as one mourns for his only son, and grieve for Him as one grieves for a firstborn" (Zechariah 12:10).

Paul's response to this revelation God gave him about Israel's future is this—Praise!

> Oh, the depth of the riches both of the wisdom and knowledge of God! How unsearchable are His judgments and His ways past finding out! ... For of Him and through Him and to Him are all things, to whom be glory forever. Amen.
> —Romans 11:33, 36

God's plan is beautiful and will be beautiful in its time. History is *His story*, and part of His story of redemption is that all Israel will be saved in such a way that God's mercy will be evident to all. Knowing God's future plan for Israel is kind of like being part of a wedding party. You know the wedding is going to be wonderful and beautiful, and your anticipation is great. You know the plan, yet you still have to work the plan. No matter what your place in the wedding ceremony, you've got to take your rightful place and fulfill your responsibilities.

You and I who know the Lord Jesus are part of the bride of Christ. We are His church, and our response to God's future restoration of Israel should mirror Paul's—the praising of our great God. No doubt it's miraculous that Israel, a nation conquered and dispersed two thousand years ago, became a nation again in 1948 out of the ashes of the Holocaust. Is God finished with Israel? No! God is working out His plan, and we as His bride are called to praise Him, communicate His plan, proclaiming His gospel to Jewish people and to all people. May our confidence in God and His promises renew and reinvigorate us. God is faithful!

Chapter 6 Study Guide

1. What are the two main themes addressed in the chapter as it relates to the book of Romans?
2. In the chapter section "Introducing Romans 9–11," how does the author organize or outline the whole book of Romans in three parts?
3. How does the author divide Romans 9–11 into three thematic parts?
4. In Romans 11:1–10 what perception did the Apostle Paul dispel regarding God's dealings with Israel? How did Paul argue his point from Jewish history?
5. According to Romans 11:11–24, what is the purpose of Israel's spiritual blindness?
6. In Romans 11:17–24, what did Paul warn gentile believers against, and why?
7. In that same section, Romans 11:17–24, what agricultural metaphors did Paul utilize in describing Jews, gentiles, and the body of Messiah, the church?
8. According to Romans 11:25–36, what is God's future plan for Israel?
9. What does Zechariah 12:10 reveal about God's future dealings with Israel?
10. What was Paul's response to the revelation of God's future plan for Israel, according to Romans 11:33, 36?

Chapter 7

The Temple, Tabernacle, and the Christian

I'm a big college football fan. In particular, I roll with the Florida Gators, as I'm an alumnus! Once, while visiting my sister in Atlanta, I went downtown and visited the College Football Hall of Fame. It was an awesome experience! I had so little time to see so many displays. There are interesting artifacts from the past, like uniforms, helmets, and footballs. My favorite parts of the museum were the pictures and movies of past games, players, and coaches! Looking at the pictures and experiencing those movies was inspiring and thrilling, to be sure, yet they were, and are, only representations of the actual reality. Those pictures and movies were real, but not the real thing. They are simply representations of that which, at a moment in time, was as real as the book or device you have in your hands.

Such were the physical tabernacle and temple, as revealed in the Word of God. Those physical structures in the Old Testament era were representations. "How?" you may wonder. In this way—they are true physical representations of spiritual reality, as we'll discover in this chapter.

As we begin our survey of the tabernacle and temple and connect the dots between the Old and New Testaments, we're also going to make powerful, poignant connections between physical and spiritual reality. There is a powerful relationship between the two, as we'll uncover in God's Word.

Once again, we start with the end in mind, as we've been doing throughout our survey of redemptive history. Jesus' person and work on behalf of mankind are front and center. The tabernacle and the temple both point to the person and work of Jesus, the Messiah, and studying them will strengthen our understanding of our great God and hopefully deepen our appreciation of His saving work—namely, His death and resurrection.

Before diving in let's discuss a big-picture concept central to our study on the tabernacle and the temple—the idea of typology. Typology is a specific kind of symbolism. A symbol is something that represents something else. Therefore, remember that the physical tabernacle and temple represent spiritual reality—that is the "something else!"

For example, Scripture identifies several Old Testament events as "types" of Christ's redemption, including the tabernacle, the sacrificial system, and the Passover. The Old Testament tabernacle is identified as a type in Hebrews 9:8–9, which says the first tabernacle was a figure for the then-present time. The high priest's entrance into the holiest place once a year prefigured the mediation of Christ, our High Priest.

Later, the veil of the tabernacle is said to be a type of Christ, in that His flesh was torn (as the veil was when He died) in order to provide entrance into God's presence for those who are covered by His sacrifice: "Therefore, brethren, having boldness to enter the Holiest by the blood of Jesus, by a new and living way which He consecrated for us, through the veil, that is, His flesh" (Hebrews 10:19–20).

The whole sacrificial system is seen as a type in Hebrews 9:19–26.

The articles of the "first testament" were dedicated with the blood of sacrifice; these articles are called "the patterns of things in the heavens" and "figures of the true."

> Therefore it was necessary that the copies of the things in the heavens should be purified with these, but the heavenly things themselves with better sacrifices than these. For Christ has not entered the holy places made with hands, which are copies of the true, but into heaven itself, now to appear in the presence of God for us.
> —Hebrews 9:23–24

This passage teaches us that the Old Testament sacrifices typify Christ's final sacrifice for the sins of the world. The Passover, as we'll study in following chapters, is also a type of Christ, according to 1 Corinthians 5:7, "… Christ, our Passover, was sacrificed for us."

The concept of "shadow" is also in the forefront, not only in our study of the tabernacle and temple. It will also be an important idea when we explore the feasts of Israel later in our journey. For example, the Apostle Paul wrote in Colossians 2:16–17, "So let no one judge you in food or in drink, or regarding a festival or a new moon or sabbaths, **which are a shadow of things to come, but the substance is of Christ."**

"Shadow" in this verse is the Greek word *skiá*—meaning the shadow of a looming presence. It also refers figuratively to a good or bad spiritual reality relating to God's light or spiritual darkness. In Colossians 2:17 that "looming presence," that reference to spiritual reality, is the "substance"—who is Christ.

Additionally, Hebrews 10:1 makes the connection between the Old Testament "shadows"—illustrated in the sacrificial system, and the New Testament "substance"—who is Christ, "For the law, having a shadow of the good things to come, and not the very image of the things, can never with these same sacrifices, which they offer continually year by year, make those who approach perfect."

With this introduction, we now have a context for our study of the tabernacle and the temple.

The Tabernacle

What was it? From the Hebrew word *mishkan*, it means "residence" or "dwelling place." It was the portable dwelling place for the divine presence of God from the time of the exodus from Egypt through the conquering of the land of Canaan. It was the central place of worship for the nation of Israel, and as such, it accompanied the Israelites on their wanderings in the wilderness and their conquest of the promised land. The first temple in Jerusalem superseded it as the dwelling place of God.

The purposes of the Tabernacle were:

» To provide a dwelling place for God—where His glory resided.
» To provide a place where God could meet with man.
» To show the "panorama of redemption."

It's first mentioned in Exodus 25:8–9 when God commanded Moses to build a tabernacle according to "the pattern" God provided: "And let them make Me a sanctuary, that I may dwell among them. According to all that I show you, that is, the pattern of the tabernacle and the pattern of all its furnishings, just so you shall make it." In Exodus 25–27 God spelled out that pattern for the tabernacle and its furnishings. These are the "blueprints."

The tabernacle was built in the fifteenth century B.C., soon after

God established the nation of Israel in the wilderness and gave them the law at Mt. Sinai. The whole tabernacle was holy in that it was set apart for worship and sacrifices to God. However, the tabernacle was separated into three areas, the outer court, the Holy Place, and the Most Holy Place (or Holy of Holies). Priests and Levites ministered in the outer court as they offered sacrifices for sin and guilt, and the other sacrifices.

- » **The Brazen Altar.** The altar was the largest piece of equipment in the tabernacle and was also known as the "altar of burnt offering" (see also Leviticus 4:7, 10, 18). It was located in the outer court. Exodus 27:1–9 provides the specific instructions God gave Moses. It was covered in bronze, and like other pieces of furniture and equipment, it was designed to be carried by poles. Bronze was a symbol of judgment, as the altar was the place where God judged sin (see also Exodus 26:31–37; Numbers 21:4–8; John 3:14–15).
- » **The Bronze Laver.** The bronze laver, also called the "bronze basin" or the "laver of brass," was also located in the outer court. It stood between the holy place and the altar, and it held water for washing (Exodus 30:18). The bronze laver was for Aaron and his sons (the priests) to wash their hands and feet before they entered the tabernacle "so that they will not die" (Exodus 30:20). The washing of the priests was to be observed by Aaron and his descendants in all ages, as long as their priesthood lasted. God wanted His people to understand the importance of purity.
- » **The Holy Place.** The Holy Place was the location of the "inner court" of the tabernacle that included the golden lampstand (Exodus 25:31–40), the table of showbread (Exodus 25:23–30), and alter of incense (Exodus 30:1–10, 34–38). The Holy Place

and the Holy of Holies were unique places that were set apart because God was uniquely present there. "Holy" simply means "set apart" or "different." God is holy, in that He is perfect in all ways, without sin. He is completely separate from sin. The golden lampstand burned continually, giving light to the Holy Place. In John 8:12, Jesus referred to Himself as "the Light of the world." Regarding the table of showbread, or table of presence, this bread was baked fresh every week, and only the priests were allowed to eat of it, as it was holy as well. Remember, Jesus declared that He was the "bread of life" in John 6:35. Lastly, the altar of incense was where special incense burned each morning and evening as an offering unto the Lord. The Holy Place was holy, or set apart, because it was a special representation and reminder of the presence of God.

» **The Holy of Holies.** The furnishing in the Holy of Holies included the ark of the covenant (Exodus 25:10–22) and the mercy seat (25:17–22).

» **The Ark of the Covenant** (also known as the Ark of Testimony) is a picture of the God-Man and also a symbol of the presence and glory of God. It originally contained the pot of manna, Aaron's rod, and the Testimony (the tablets containing the Ten Commandments). Hebrews 9:3–4 reiterates this truth, "and behind the second veil, the part of the tabernacle which is called the Holiest of All, which had the golden censer and the ark of the covenant overlaid on all sides with gold, in which were the golden pot that had the manna, Aaron's rod that budded, and the tablets of the covenant."

» **The Pot of Manna** (Exodus 25:10–18, 26:31–34) represented God's provision for His people. The pot was round, representing eternality, and it was gold, indicating divinity. This points to Jesus, who declared, "... I am the bread of life. He who comes to Me shall never hunger, and he who believes in Me shall never thirst" (John 6:35).

- **Aaron's rod** represented the priesthood (Numbers 17:2–10) and was a testimony of God's choice of Moses and Aaron to lead His people. Priests served as mediators between God and men. Aaron was the first high priest. Hebrews 9:11–15 affirms the person and work of the Great High Priest, Jesus:

> But Christ came as High Priest of the good things to come, with the greater and more perfect tabernacle not made with hands, that is, not of this creation. Not with the blood of goats and calves, but with His own blood He entered the Most Holy Place once for all, having obtained eternal redemption. For if the blood of bulls and goats and the ashes of a heifer, sprinkling the unclean, sanctifies for the purifying of the flesh, how much more shall the blood of Christ, who through the eternal Spirit offered Himself without spot to God, cleanse your conscience from dead works to serve the living God? And for this reason He is the Mediator of the new covenant, by means of death, for the redemption of the transgressions under the first covenant, that those who are called may receive the promise of the eternal inheritance.

- **The Testimony** (Exodus 25:16) included the two stone tablets containing the Ten Commandments. We see the obvious fulfillment of the Testimony in the living word of God, Jesus, "In the beginning was the Word, and the Word was with God, and the Word was God. ... And the Word became flesh and dwelt among us, and we beheld His glory, the glory as of the only begotten of the Father, full of grace and truth" (John 1:1, 14). The tabernacle was a place where God's glory was revealed. In a similar fashion, God's glory was revealed through and in the person of Messiah Jesus.

» **The Mercy Seat** (Exodus 25:17) was the lid or cover of the ark, the place where atonement took place. Between the Shekinah glory cloud above the ark and the tablets of law inside the ark was the blood-sprinkled cover. Blood from the sacrifices stood between God and the broken law of God!

As we conclude this section on the tabernacle, we're reminded how the magnificent physical tabernacle represented the spiritual reality found in our Great High Priest Jesus, who not only died and rose again that sinful man might be reconciled to God by faith, but He continues to minister in that heavenly tabernacle on behalf of His people. Hebrews 8:1–6 wonderfully sums up this survey of the tabernacle and work of the high priest:

> Now this is the main point of the things we are saying: We have such a High Priest, who is seated at the right hand of the throne of the Majesty in the heavens, a Minister of the sanctuary and of the true tabernacle which the Lord erected, and not man. For every high priest is appointed to offer both gifts and sacrifices. Therefore it is necessary that this One also have something to offer. For if He were on earth, He would not be a priest, since there are priests who offer the gifts according to the law; who serve the copy and shadow of the heavenly things, as Moses was divinely instructed when he was about to make the tabernacle. For He said, "See that you make all things according to the pattern shown you on the mountain." But now He has obtained a more excellent ministry, inasmuch as He is also Mediator of a better covenant, which was established on better promises.

The Temple

While the tabernacle was portable, the temple was a permanent, stationary structure, located in Jerusalem, the "City of God" (Psalm 48:1, 8). Like the tabernacle, it was also a house for the Lord. While King David desired and intended to build the temple, it was his son, Solomon, who actually built the temple. First Chronicles 22:1–11 explains from David's perspective:

> Then David said, "This is the house of the Lord God, and this is the altar of burnt offering for Israel." So David commanded to gather the aliens who were in the land of Israel; and he appointed masons to cut hewn stones to build the house of God. And David prepared iron in abundance for the nails of the doors of the gates and for the joints, and bronze in abundance beyond measure, and cedar trees in abundance; for the Sidonians and those from Tyre brought much cedar wood to David. Now David said, "Solomon my son is young and inexperienced, and the house to be built for the Lord must be exceedingly magnificent, famous and glorious throughout all countries. I will now make preparation for it." So David made abundant preparations before his death. Then he called for his son Solomon, and charged him to build a house for the Lord God of Israel. And David said to Solomon: "My son, as for me, it was in my mind to build a house to the name of the Lord my God; but the word of the Lord came to me, saying, 'You have shed much blood and have made great wars; you shall not build a house for My name, because you have shed much blood on the earth in My sight. Behold, a son shall be born to you, who shall be a man of rest; and I will give him rest from all his enemies all around. His name shall be Solomon, for I will give peace and quietness to Israel

in his days. He shall build a house for My name, and he shall be My son, and I will be his Father; and I will establish the throne of his kingdom over Israel forever.' Now, my son, may the Lord be with you; and may you prosper, and build the house of the Lord your God, as He has said to you."

Second Chronicles 2:1–9 provides a glimpse from Solomon's point of view:

> Then Solomon determined to build a temple for the name of the Lord, and a royal house for himself. Solomon selected seventy thousand men to bear burdens, eighty thousand to quarry stone in the mountains, and three thousand six hundred to oversee them. Then Solomon sent to Hiram king of Tyre, saying: As you have dealt with David my father, and sent him cedars to build himself a house to dwell in, so deal with me. Behold, I am building a temple for the name of the Lord my God, to dedicate it to Him, to burn before Him sweet incense, for the continual showbread, for the burnt offerings morning and evening, on the Sabbaths, on the New Moons, and on the set feasts of the Lord our God. This is an ordinance forever to Israel. And the temple which I build will be great, for our God is greater than all gods. But who is able to build Him a temple, since heaven and the heaven of heavens cannot contain Him? Who am I then, that I should build Him a temple, except to burn sacrifice before Him? Therefore send me at once a man skillful to work in gold and silver, in bronze and iron, in purple and crimson and blue, who has skill to engrave with the skillful men who are with me in Judah and Jerusalem, whom David my father provided. Also send me cedar and cypress and algum logs from Lebanon, for I know that your servants have skill to cut timber in

Lebanon; and indeed my servants will be with your servants, to prepare timber for me in abundance, for the temple which I am about to build shall be great and wonderful.

The temple provided a place for God's people to go and offer sacrifices of worship to the Lord. Like the tabernacle, the temple was the place where God's glory dwelt, the place where men worshipped God, the place where sacrifices were offered, and the place where atonement was accomplished.

The first temple, also known as Solomon's Temple, was completed in 957 B.C. According to 1 Kings 6–7, the temple building endeavor began four hundred and eighty years after the exodus from Egypt and took seven years to complete. Solomon's temple was destroyed in 587–586 B.C. by the king of Babylon, Nebuchadnezzar II. Subsequently, it was rebuilt by the Jewish people, the work being completed in 515 B.C. with the blessing of King Cyrus II of Persia, who allowed the exiled Jewish people to return to Jerusalem and restore the walls of the city along with the temple structure itself.

New Testament Connections

Spiritual connections between the tabernacle, the temple, and Christians are replete throughout the New Testament.

Regarding the tabernacle, just as God tabernacled, or dwelt, among His people during Israel's time in the wilderness, the Lord also tabernacled with us through the person of Christ Jesus, "And the Word became flesh and dwelt [tabernacled] among us, and we beheld His glory, the glory as of the only begotten of the Father, full of grace and truth" (John 1:14).

Ultimately, He's going to tabernacle with His people, the church, in heaven forever. As Revelation 21:2–4 declares:

> Then I, John, saw the holy city, New Jerusalem, coming down out of heaven from God, prepared as a bride adorned for her husband. And I heard a loud voice from heaven saying, "Behold, the tabernacle of God is with men, and He will dwell with them, and they shall be His people. God Himself will be with them and be their God. And God will wipe away every tear from their eyes; there shall be no more death, nor sorrow, nor crying. There shall be no more pain, for the former things have passed away."

The Apostle Paul referred to individual Christians as temples of the Holy Spirit twice in the book of First Corinthians:

> Do you not know that you are the temple of God and that the Spirit of God dwells in you? If anyone defiles the temple of God, God will destroy him. For the temple of God is holy, which temple you are.
> —1 Corinthians 3:16–17

> Or do you not know that your body is the temple of the Holy Spirit who is in you, whom you have from God, and you are not your own?
> —1 Corinthians 6:19

The moment we place our trust and faith in Jesus Christ as our Savior, the Holy Spirit, the *Ruach Ha'Kadosh* in Hebrew, indwells the believer, as 1 Corinthians 12:13 teaches. Now God's presence, His glory, in the person of the Holy Spirit, no longer fills a location. Rather, He now indwells flesh and bones, namely human beings who trust in Christ. What a beautiful reality!

There's more. While Paul explained the individual nature of people as temples of the Holy Spirit, there is a corporate relationship between the Lord and His people. Ephesians 2:19–21 reveals that the church is the temple of God in a corporate sense:

> Now, therefore, you are no longer strangers and foreigners, but fellow citizens with the saints and members of the household of God, having been built on the foundation of the apostles and prophets, Jesus Christ Himself being the chief cornerstone, in whom the whole building, being fitted together, grows into a holy temple in the Lord.

Finally, there's a heavenly connection to the temple, God, and His people. There is a temple in Heaven, as the book of Revelation reveals. Here are just a few references:

> Then the temple of God was opened in heaven, and the ark of His covenant was seen in His temple. And there were lightnings, noises, thunderings, an earthquake, and great hail.
> —Revelation 11:19

> Then another angel came out of the temple which is in heaven, he also having a sharp sickle.
> —Revelation 14:17

> After these things I looked, and behold, the temple of the tabernacle of the testimony in heaven was opened.
> —Revelation 15:5

> The temple was filled with smoke from the glory of God and from

His power, and no one was able to enter the temple till the seven plagues of the seven angels were completed.
—Revelation 15:8

While these passages affirm there is a temple in heaven, ultimately, the eternal temple is not a structure. Rather, it is the Lord Himself. When the recorded history of man comes to a close (in Revelation 21:1), God will work a complete make-over of heaven and earth (Isaiah 65:17; 2 Peter 3:12–13). The new heaven and new earth are what some theologians call the "eternal state" and will be "where righteousness dwells" (2 Peter 3:13). After the re-creation God will reveal the New Jerusalem, as John saw a glimpse of it in his vision: "And he carried me away in the Spirit to a great and high mountain, and showed me the great city, the holy Jerusalem, descending out of heaven from God, having the glory of God …" (Revelation 21:10–11).

This is the city that Abraham looked for by faith (Hebrews 11:10). It is the place God will dwell with His people forever (Revelation 21:3), and it is the place whose inhabitants will have all their tears wiped away (Revelation 21:4).

John described the temple in the New Jerusalem:

But I saw no temple in it, for the Lord God Almighty and the Lamb are its temple. The city had no need of the sun or of the moon to shine in it, for the glory of God illuminated it. The Lamb is its light. And the nations of those who are saved shall walk in its light, and the kings of the earth bring their glory and honor into it.
—Revelation 21:22–24

Praise be to our great God, who is worthy of all praise, honor, majesty, and power, full of wisdom and truth! Amen!

Chapter 7 Study Guide

1. What is biblical typology? Why is it germane to our study of the tabernacle and temple?
2. According to Colossians 2:16–17 and Hebrews 10:1, compare the biblical concepts of "shadow" and "substance"? Why is it important to distinguish between them?
3. What was the tabernacle? What were its main purposes?
4. What were the basic furnishings that made up the tabernacle (i.e., brazen altar), and what purpose did each have?
5. According to Hebrews 8:1–6, who is the great High Priest and where is He ministering?
6. How were the tabernacle and temple similar, and how were they different?
7. Describe the roles of both David and Solomon in the planning and construction of the temple.
8. According to 1 Corinthians 3:16–17 and 1 Corinthians 6:19, how does the Word of God describe believers in Jesus?
9. In Ephesians 2:19–21, how does Paul describe the relationship between God and His people, the church?
10. How does the book of Revelation describe the temple in heaven?

Chapter 8

Passover and Pentecost

Signposts are integral to navigating life in our modern world, as they support our quest to get from point A to point B. Sometimes those signposts are directional. Other times they may be mile markers. In any case, without signposts our efforts to understand where we are in relation to where we are going will be greatly hampered, and our ability to reach our destination will be diminished, if not sabotaged completely. With the support of signposts, we can arrive at our intended destination and engage the purpose for which that destination was designed—be it business, pleasure, or otherwise.

As we ponder our journey down redemption road through our biblical survey of redemptive history, we come to the feasts of Israel. These feasts of Israel, germane to ancient Israel historically and to the Jewish people today, also have profound significance to mankind in general and to the church specifically. The feasts of Israel are in one sense, spiritual signposts that say, "This way to Messiah." As we embark on this brief journey through the feasts of Israel, we will discover that they powerfully point to the person and work of Jesus.

The feasts of Israel find their fulfillment in Jesus and the ultimate spiritual destination of salvation. A study of them will not only help us better understand God's dealings with Israel but will help us better understand God's plan of salvation. As Romans 10:9–10 declares, "that if you confess with your mouth the Lord Jesus and believe in your heart that God has raised Him from the dead, you will be saved. For with the heart one believes unto righteousness, and with the mouth confession is made unto salvation."

The feasts point to Jesus, who has made the way of salvation possible. As He proclaimed about Himself in John 14:6, "… I am the way, the truth, and the life. No one comes to the Father except through Me."

In this chapter we'll introduce the feasts of Israel and focus our specific study on Passover and Shavuot (Pentecost)—the two major spring festivals. In chapter 9, we'll then turn our attention to the fall feasts of Israel—the Feast of Trumpets (Rosh Hashanna), the Day of Atonement (Yom Kippur), and the Feast of Tabernacles (Sukkot).

Yes, the feasts of Israel are the signs that lead to salvation. While they were originally established as God's appointed times for the Jewish people, they are of great importance to all people, including believers in Jesus Christ, as we'll discover at our latest stop on Redemption Road.

God's Appointed Times

If you're a believer in Jesus Christ, you're familiar with the concept of individual quiet times with the Lord. The Lord gave ancient Israel what we might call corporate quiet times—God's appointed times.

Our study of the feasts of Israel begins in Leviticus 23:1–2: "And the Lord spoke to Moses, saying, "Speak to the children of Israel, and say to them: 'The feasts of the Lord, which you shall proclaim to be holy convocations, these are My feasts.'" The Hebrew word used here for feasts is the word moed, which means "appointed time," a time for people to stop everything and focus their attention on

God—who He is and what He has done for them.

As the church, we have times of corporate worship, like Sunday morning, and as individual Christians we have "quiet times" with the Lord. In ancient Israel these feasts were not feasts in the modern sense of banquets and celebrations, but rather were based on the altar of sacrifice and God's covenant relationship with Israel.

The first of these appointed times is the Sabbath, a weekly reminder of God's creation of the world and of His covenant with Israel. As Leviticus 23:3 states, "'Six days shall work be done, but the seventh day is a Sabbath of solemn rest, a holy convocation. You shall do no work on it; it is the Sabbath of the Lord in all your dwellings."

Because of the limited scope of our study, we won't delve into the Sabbath. With Christians having varied views and many questions surrounding the Sabbath, I will recommend the book *Christ in the Sabbath* by Rich Robinson. It is an excellent resource on the Sabbath and how it relates to the Christian today.

Following the Sabbath, the other seven annual feasts fall naturally into two distinct groups. The first four of these occur in the spring and are all related to the Passover. The last three all take place during the seventh month of the Hebrew calendar, the sacred month of Tishri, and are known as the fall feasts of Israel.

In this Chapter, we'll focus on the feasts of Israel that occur in the spring—Passover, Unleavened Bread, and Shavuot (Pentecost). In Chapter 9, we'll turn our attention to the fall feasts of Israel—Rosh Hashanah (also known as the Feasts of Trumpets), Yom Kippur, the Day of Atonement, and Sukkot (also called the Feast of Tabernacles or Booths).

The ancient Hebrews observed a twelve-month lunar calendar based on Psalm 104:19, where the scripture states, "He appointed the moon for the seasons; The sun knows its going down." Ancient

Israel had elaborate protocols in place to precisely determine the new moon so that the appointed times or feasts could be observed on the correct days.

The first appointed time on the annual religious calendar was Passover.

Passover

In their tremendous book, *Christ in the Passover*, Ceil and Moishe Rosen describe Passover as "God's Object Lesson."

Leviticus 23:5–8 introduces for us Passover and the Feast of Unleavened Bread,

> On the fourteenth day of the first month at twilight is the Lord's Passover. And on the fifteenth day of the same month is the Feast of Unleavened Bread to the Lord; seven days you must eat unleavened bread. On the first day you shall have a holy convocation; you shall do no customary work on it. But you shall offer an offering made by fire to the Lord for seven days. The seventh day shall be a holy convocation; you shall do no customary work on it.

In Exodus 12:1–20 God provides more specific Passover details. Verses 3–7 detail the sacrifice of the Passover Lamb:

> Speak to all the congregation of Israel, saying: "On the tenth of this month every man shall take for himself a lamb, according to the house of his father, a lamb for a household. And if the household is too small for the lamb, let him and his neighbor next to his house take it according to the number of the persons; according to each man's need you shall make your count for the lamb. Your lamb

shall be without blemish, a male of the first year. You may take it from the sheep or from the goats. Now you shall keep it until the fourteenth day of the same month. Then the whole assembly of the congregation of Israel shall kill it at twilight. And they shall take some of the blood and put it on the two doorposts and on the lintel of the houses where they eat it."

The innocent Passover lamb foreshadowed the One who would arrive centuries later to be God's final means of redemption and atonement.

The Fulfillment in Jesus. Some people may ask, "What's Jesus have to do with Passover? Passover is Jewish." Well, so was Jesus. He was Jewish and celebrated Passover every year while He lived on this Earth as a man, but His connection is so much more! As John declared in John 1:29, "... Behold! The Lamb of God who takes away the sin of the world!"

Just as the Passover lamb was marked for death, so was Jesus. As Isaiah 53:7 states about the sacrifice of Messiah, "He was led as a lamb to the slaughter."

Additionally, note that the Passover lamb was "without blemish." First Peter 1:18–19 states that the believers in Jesus are "... not redeemed with corruptible things, like silver or gold, from your aimless conduct received by tradition from your fathers, but with the precious blood of Christ, **as of a lamb without blemish and without spot.**

Covered by the blood. The Israelites had to place the blood on the doorposts of their homes by faith, so when the angel of death came, he would "pass over" those covered by the blood,

"For I will pass through the land of Egypt on that night, and will strike all the firstborn in the land of Egypt, both man and beast; and against all the gods of Egypt I will execute judgment: I am the LORD. Now the blood shall be a sign for you on the houses where you are. And when I see the blood, I will pass over you; and the plague shall not be on you to destroy you when I strike the land of Egypt."

—Exodus 12:12–13

Just as the ancient Israelites had to apply in faith the blood of the lamb to the doorposts of their homes to escape physical death, so human beings must place, by faith, the blood of the Messiah Jesus to the doorposts of our hearts to escape spiritual death, which is eternal separation from God in hell. What a mighty act of redemption the Lord has accomplished!

The unleavened bread. Unleavened bread was an important component of the Passover meal, as God commanded the Israelites to eat the Passover lamb with "unleavened bread" (Exodus 12:8).

They ate the unleavened bread in haste, because they would be leaving Egypt quickly during the exodus, but there's more. Leaven in the scriptures is usually a symbol of sin, therefore the putting away of all leaven would have been a picture of the cleansing from sin. Passover and the Feast of Unleavened Bread (seven days following Passover) would be an everlasting memorial given to the Israelites. As Exodus 12:14–15 declared, "So this day shall be to you a memorial; and you shall keep it as a feast to the LORD throughout your generations. You shall keep it as a feast by an everlasting ordinance."

The Israelites were to be consecrated, set apart, unto the Lord. The unleavened bread at Passover in the Passover observance for generations going forward would be a powerful reminder. Unleavened bread in a spiritual sense is a picture of a sinless nature. Jesus, the

Bread of Life, was perfect, sinless. Just as the unleavened bread pictured being freed from physical bondage in Egypt for the Israelites, so God's people, the church, are to be pure, "unleavened," for we have been delivered from the spiritual bondage of sin through the sacrifice of the perfect Lamb of God, Jesus. As the Apostle Paul noted, in 1 Corinthians 5:6–7: "Do you not know that a little leaven leavens the whole lump? Therefore purge out the old leaven, that you may be a new lump, since you truly are unleavened. For indeed Christ, our Passover, was sacrificed for us. "

We've only scratched the surface regarding Passover and Jesus, touching only on a few highlights. For a more detailed study, I recommend to you the excellent book previously mentioned, *Christ in the Passover*, by Ceil and Moishe Rosen. This tremendous primer not only makes more biblical connections to Christ, but it also elaborates on how many of the cultural elements of the Passover and Seder meal today point to the person and work of Messiah Jesus.

As His people, may we praise God each and every day for the provision of our Passover Lamb, Jesus, our Savior and Lord!

Shavuot

Shavuot occurs seven sabbaths and a day (fifty days) after Passover. This feast is also called the "Firstfruits" or the "Feast of Weeks." The Hebrew word *Shavuot* means "weeks" or "sevens" because we count seven sevens from the day after Passover. Christians are familiar with the Greek word *Pentecost*, which literally means "fiftieth." These different names for this feast—Shavuot, Pentecost, the Feast of Weeks, or the Firstfruits—are synonymous, and all refer to the fifty-day period after Passover culminating with the day the feast is celebrated. Shavuot was a time for the Israelites to give thanks to

God for their produce during the barley season.

Firstfruits also provided an opportunity for Israel to trust God rather than Baal and the other Canaanite nature gods and was a reminder to them that the Lord was their Creator and Provider. Additionally, according to Jewish tradition, God gave Moses the law on Mt. Sinai during Shavuot.

Shavuot was one of three feasts requiring all Jewish men to make a pilgrimage to Jerusalem. Passover and the Feast of Tabernacles were the other two (see also Exodus 34:23). As Deuteronomy 16:16 states: "Three times a year all your males shall appear before the LORD your God in the place which He chooses: at the Feast of Unleavened Bread, at the Feast of Weeks, and at the Feast of Tabernacles; and they shall not appear before the LORD empty-handed."

Christians may not know the birthday of the church at Pentecost in Acts 2 occurred on the Jewish Feast of Shavuot! As Acts 2:1–4 reveals:

> When the Day of Pentecost had fully come, they were all with one accord in one place. And suddenly there came a sound from heaven, as of a rushing mighty wind, and it filled the whole house where they were sitting. Then there appeared to them divided tongues, as of fire, and one sat upon each of them. And they were all filled with the Holy Spirit and began to speak with other tongues, as the Spirit gave them utterance.

In the last chapter of our study, we'll do a deeper study of Acts 2. For now, note the connection between the birthday of the church and the Feast of Shavuot, Pentecost. While Shavuot, or Pentecost, was an annual feast on the Jewish religious calendar, the coming of the Spirit and birth of the church in Acts 2 was a singular event, which occurred on the feast day, for many reasons we'll discover. In short, both the agricultural feast day of Shavuot and the coming of the Spirit at Pentecost are both about harvest—manifested by God's blessing, God's power, and God's provision. There is a physical harvest, yes, but there is also a spiritual harvest.

God instituted the Feast of Weeks in Leviticus 23:15–22:

> And you shall count for yourselves from the day after the Sabbath, from the day that you brought the sheaf of the wave offering: seven Sabbaths shall be completed. Count fifty days to the day after the seventh Sabbath; then you shall offer a new grain offering to the Lord. You shall bring from your dwellings two wave loaves of two-tenths of an ephah. They shall be of fine flour; they shall be baked with leaven. They are the firstfruits to the Lord. And you shall offer with the bread seven lambs of the first year, without blemish, one young bull, and two rams. They shall be as a burnt offering to the Lord, with their grain offering and their drink offerings, an offering made by fire for a sweet aroma to the Lord. Then you shall sacrifice one kid of the goats as a sin offering, and two male lambs of the first year as a sacrifice of a peace offering. The priest shall wave them with the bread of the firstfruits as a wave offering before the Lord, with the two lambs. They shall be holy to the Lord for the priest. And you shall proclaim on the same day that it is a holy convocation to you. You shall do no customary work on it. It shall be a statute forever in all your dwellings throughout your generations. "When you reap the harvest of your land, you shall not wholly reap the corners of your field when you reap, nor shall you gather any gleaning from your harvest. You shall leave them for the poor and for the stranger: I am the Lord your God."

"Firstfruits" and "harvest "are the key words from this passage that will strengthen our understanding. Leviticus 23:17 states, "You shall bring from your dwellings two wave loaves of two-tenths of an ephah. They shall be of fine flour; they shall be baked with leaven. They are the firstfruits to the Lord." Here in Leviticus 23 the word firsfruits is associated with physical harvest. In Acts 2 there was a spiritual component, as there was a harvest of three thousand souls (Acts 2:38–41), people who responded to Peter's preaching and were saved following the Spirit falling upon him and the other disciples.

Shavuot, as we've mentioned, is also called the Feast of Firstfruits. "And you shall observe the Feast of Weeks, of the firstfruits of wheat harvest …" (Exodus 34:22). The most common Hebrew word for "firstfruits" is *bikkurim*. Once firstfruits were offered to the Lord, the rest could be utilized by the farmer.

Additionally, in the Torah (the five books of Moses), the idea of firstfruits was connected to the principle of the firstborn: "Consecrate to Me all the firstborn, whatever opens the womb among the children of Israel, both of man and beast; it is Mine" (Exodus 13:2).

In the same way, the Lord told the people that the firstfruits of the ground also belong to Him, "Honor the Lord with your possessions, And with the firstfruits of all your increase; So your barns will be filled with plenty, And your vats will overflow with new wine" (Proverbs 3:9–10).

One application for the follower of Jesus is that this feast speaks of the importance of dedicating our first and our best to God's glory. This may include our time, talents, and other resources—all gifts and blessings from the Lord. Honoring the Lord with our firstfruits is part of the dedication and trust He expects and deserves.

Spiritual Firstfruits in the New Testament

The spiritual concept of firstfruits in the New Testament is very important for the follower of Messiah Jesus. The Greek word for firstfruits is *aparche*, found nine times in the New Testament, seven of those times in the Pauline epistles. *Aparche* is defined as:

1. to offer firstlings or firstfruits; and
2. to take away the firstfruits of the productions of the earth, which were offered to God.

Paul used the image of firstfruits to refer to the resurrected Jesus, the first believers in a particular geographical area, and the Holy Spirit. In 1 Corinthians 15:22–23, Jesus is called the Firstfruits: "For as in Adam all die, even so in Christ all shall be made alive. But each one in his own order: **Christ the firstfruits,** afterward those who are Christ's at His coming." Just as the firstfruits came before the rest of the crop, so Jesus rose as the first of a greater harvest to come, namely His children, Christians. And just as firstfruits was a type of guarantee or down payment for the fuller harvest, so the resurrection of Jesus guarantees that we who have received Him will likewise be resurrected.

Paul also applied the firstfruits metaphor to the Holy Spirit, stating, "Not only that, but we also who have **the firstfruits of the Spirit,** even we ourselves groan within ourselves, eagerly waiting for the adoption, the redemption of our body" (Romans 8:23).

Lastly, James applied this term "firstfruits" to all believers, "Of His own will He brought us forth by the word of truth, that we might be **a kind of firstfruits of His creatures"** (James 1:18). Here James used the term "firstfruits" to describe all believers as the first element in the final redemption that will come to the entire universe. Once again, we see the firstfruits as the beginning of God's provision, with the promise of more to come.

As we've seen repeatedly in the Hebrew scriptures (i.e., our study of the tabernacle and temple), a physical essence points to a spiritual reality that culminates in the person and work of Messiah. Hallelujah!

"Oh, give thanks to the Lord! Call upon His name; Make known His deeds among the peoples! Sing to Him, sing psalms to Him; Talk of all His wondrous works! Glory in His holy name …" (Psalm 105:1–3).

Go, Receive, Witness

Followers of Jesus Christ need to understand the powerful connection between Passover, Shavuot and the great commission! The singular event in Acts 2, the birth of the church on Shavuot, otherwise known as Pentecost, was unique. There was not a Shavuot like it prior to the event recorded in scripture, nor would there be a Shavuot like it going forward.

As Jesus was preparing the disciples for ministry following His ascension, He taught them about the spiritual harvest of souls. When the resurrected Jesus gave them their marching orders in Matthew 28:18–20, the primary directive was to "go and make disciples,"

> And Jesus came and spoke to them, saying, "All authority has been given to Me in heaven and on earth. Go therefore and make disciples of all the nations, baptizing them in the name of the Father and of the Son and of the Holy Spirit, teaching them to observe all things that I have commanded you; and lo, I am with you always, even to the end of the age." Amen.
>
> —Matthew 28:18–20

And immediately before His ascension, He promised they would receive the power to witness to the end of the earth, "But you shall receive power when the Holy Spirit has come upon you; and you shall be witnesses to Me in Jerusalem, and in all Judea and Samaria, and to the end of the earth." (Acts 1:8).

Just like sowing seed and working in a physical field required faith and trust for God to provide the blessing, so it would be in the spiritual field.

As the disciples were empowered by the Spirit and proclaimed the good news about the person and work of Y'shua, "the Lamb of God who takes away the sin of the world" (John 1:29), the Lord brought about the great harvest of souls. Jesus taught on the spiritual harvest in Matthew 9:37–38 when He declared, "... The harvest truly is plentiful, but the laborers are few. Therefore pray the Lord of the harvest to send out laborers into His harvest."

In John 4:35–36 the Lord used the agricultural motif in describing the spiritual harvest, "... Behold, I say to you, lift up your eyes and look at the fields, for they are already white for harvest! And he who reaps receives wages, and gathers fruit for eternal life, that both he who sows and he who reaps may rejoice together."

As His children, we're not only answers to that two thousand-year-old prayer, we are the harvest. We're also laborers in the field that continues to be before us in this present day, the Church Age. May we be found faithful in working God's field through prayer, good works, and gospel proclamation—declaring the Passover Lamb, Jesus, through the power granted those first disciples at Pentecost, the Holy Spirit. The harvest is truly plentiful. Amen.

Chapter 8 Study Guide

1. How does Leviticus 23:1–2 describe the feasts of Israel? What was the general purpose of the feasts as it related to God and His people?
2. In your own words, how would you explain Passover?
3. According to Exodus 12:3–7, what kind of lamb was to be sacrificed at Passover, and what was to be done with its blood? In John 1:29 how does John the Baptist describe Y'shua (Jesus)?
4. According to Exodus 12:12–13, what is the circumstance surrounding the origin of the name Passover (*Pesach* in Hebrew)?
5. What is the connection between the slain Passover lambs and the sacrifice of Christ?
6. How long after Passover does the Feast of Weeks, also known as Shavuot or Pentecost, occur? In simple terms, what were the Jewish people celebrating during the feast?
7. In one word, what was the shared principle between the typical feast of Shavuot and Pentecost, the birthday of the church? Hint: one was physical, the other spiritual, in nature.
8. How and where is the spiritual motif of "firstfruits" used in the New Testament?
9. How did Jesus use the agricultural motif of harvest in an evangelistic sense in both Matthew 9:37–38 and John 4:35–36?
10. We understand the harvest of souls to which Jesus referred in the gospels, but how do we sow and water evangelistically in our daily walk as we desire that people come to a saving knowledge of Jesus?

Chapter 9

The Fall Feasts of Israel

We all like vacation getaways. We've all prepared for trips to desired destinations. Some preparations are more complicated and involved than others, yet the goal is the same—to arrive at the locale we've fancied, then enjoy all the benefits that place affords.

It's been said that a journey of a thousand miles begins with a step. As we travel down Redemption Road, we come to a culmination of sorts as we approach the fall feasts of Israel. They are in order of observance: Rosh Hashanah, also known as the Feasts of Trumpets; Yom Kippur, the Day of Atonement; and Sukkot, also called the Feast of Tabernacles or Booths.

As part of that spiritual culmination on the Jewish religious calendar, there are powerful threads of redemption with which the Christian can identify. These concepts will help us not only grow in our understanding of the person and work of Messiah Jesus, but will help us better appreciate the salvation we have through faith in Christ, our Lord.

Before we dive into the fall feasts in particular, I want us to review this reality: each of the feasts of Israel find their ultimate fulfillment in the work of Messiah Jesus.

As we noted in Chapter 8, our study of the feasts of Israel began in Leviticus 23:1–2,

"And the Lord spoke to Moses, saying, 'Speak to the children of Israel, and say to them: "The feasts of the Lord, which you shall proclaim to be holy convocations, these are My feasts."'"

If you remember, the Hebrew word used here for "feasts" is the word *moed* which means "appointed time," a time for people to stop everything and focus their attention on God, who He is and what He has done for them.

The chart below shows God's institution of the feasts in Leviticus 23 along with corresponding New Testament passages highlighting their fulfillment in Messiah Jesus. A study of the material scriptures below will enhance understanding of the flow from Old Testament feast to New Testament fulfillment. Note the verses from Leviticus 23 are listed along with the general dates on our Gregorian (Christian or Western) calendar when the feasts occur.

Messiah Fulfills Israel's Feasts

The Feasts (Leviticus 23)	Messiah's Fulfillment
Passover (March/April)—Lev. 23:4–8 (read also Exod. 12:1–20)	Death of Messiah—1 Cor. 5:7; John 1:29
Unleavened Bread (March/April)—seven-day holiday	Sinlessness of Messiah—1 Peter 2:22; 2 Cor. 5:21)
Firstfruits (March/April)—Lev. 23:9–14	Resurrection of Messiah—1 Cor. 15:23
Feast of Weeks (May/June)—Lev. 23:15–21 (see also Acts 2)	Outpouring of the Spirit of Messiah—Acts 1:5; 2:4
Feast of Trumpets (Sept./Oct.)—Lev. 23:23–25	Second Coming of Messiah—1 Thess. 4:16–17; 1 Cor. 15:52

The Feasts (Leviticus 23)	Messiah's Fulfillment
Day of Atonement (Sept./Oct.)—Lev. 23:26–32	Substitutionary sacrifice by Messiah—Hebrews 9:28
Feast of Booths (Sept./Oct.)—Lev. 23:33–34, 39–43 (Millennial Kingdom)	Rest and reunion with Messiah—Zechariah 14:16–19

To review, remember also that the ancient Hebrews observed a twelve-month lunar calendar based on Psalm 104:19, where the scripture states, " He appointed the moon for seasons; The sun knows its going down." They had elaborate protocol in place to precisely determine the new moon, so that the appointed times, or feasts, could be observed on the correct days.

The fall feasts of Israel occur in the seventh month on the Hebrew calendar, the sacred month of Tishri. The reason Tishri is called the "sacred month" is because it's the seventh month on the Jewish calendar, and seven, as you may know, symbolizes divine perfection. It also contains the most holy days of any month on the Jewish calendar—hence the connection with culmination. Additionally, Tishri is the sabbatical month, and along with the seventh day of the week, was set apart as sacred.

The fall feasts are unique among God's appointed times because they form a natural progression of thought. Mitch and Zhava Glaser note in their superb book, *The Fall Feasts of Israel*:

> The Feast of Trumpets (Rosh Hashanah) teaches repentance; Yom Kippur, the Day of Atonement, redemption; and Sukkot, the Feast of Tabernacles or Booths, rejoicing. On the Feast of Trumpets, the sound of the ram's horn calls upon each Jew to repent and confess his sins before his Maker. The Day of Atonement is that ominous

day when peace is made with God. On the Feast of Tabernacles, Israel obeys God's command to rejoice over the harvest and the goodness of God. It's necessary to pass through repentance and redemption in order to experience His joy."[10]

Now that we have our itinerary for this incredible stop on our journey down Redemption Road, let's begin our excursion by delving into the Feast of Trumpets.

The Feast of Trumpets—Rosh Hashanah

God instituted this feast in Leviticus 23:23–25:

> Then the LORD spoke to Moses, saying, "Speak to the children of Israel, saying: 'In the seventh month, on the first day of the month, you shall have a sabbath-rest, a memorial of blowing of trumpets, a holy convocation. You shall do no customary work on it; and you shall offer an offering made by fire to the LORD.'"

The Feast of Trumpets, more commonly called Rosh Hashanah, marks the beginning of the civil year and is the Jewish New Year's Day. This day begins what are known as the ten "days of awe," a time when Jewish people examine their lives and repent of sins. When God gave the calendar of feasts to Israel, this feast wasn't originally named. In Hebrew it was simply called *Yom Truah*, the day of blowing, the blowing of the trumpets. Why did the Lord institute this feast? He wanted to commemorate this sacred season with a trumpet blast to get the people's attention!

---

10. *The Fall Feasts of Israel* by Mitch and Zhava Glaser; pg. 16; Copyright 1987; The Moody Bible Institute of Chicago; Moody Press-Publisher

Three things are traditionally observed on Rosh Hashanah. First, it's a celebration of the New Year. You may wonder, "How can Rosh Hashanah be the New Year and occur in the seventh month?" That's a good question. Rosh Hashanah literally means "head of the year" and marks the beginning of the civil year, not the biblical or religious year, which begins in the spring. A second prominent tradition on Rosh Hashanah is to remember Abraham's binding of Isaac and God's provision of the ram for sacrifice. A third tradition is the blowing of the shofar. The blowing of the shofar is a call to repentance, and it's also a reminder of God's covenant made with Israel at Mt. Sinai. The blowing of the shofar marks the beginning of the days of awe, a time of preparation of the heart for Yom Kippur.

The real theme of Rosh Hashanah is repentance. The Gemara, a collection of rabbinic thought on Judaism put together between the third and fifth centuries, states:

> Three books are opened on Rosh Hashanah, one for the completely righteous, one for the completely wicked, and one for the average persons. The completely righteous are immediately inscribed in the book of life. The completely wicked are immediately inscribed in the book of death. The average persons are kept in suspension from Rosh Hashanah to Yom Kippur.[11]

As you can imagine, most people fall into the "average" person category, not knowing exactly where they stand with God! During these ten days, traditional Jewish observers try to tip the scales in their favor so they can be inscribed in the book of life. *Mitzvot*, or good deeds, are done, like giving to the poor. Confessions are recited, and differences with others are resolved. The ceremony of *Tashlich*, the

---

11. Ibid, pg. 33.

symbolic casting of sins into the water, follows afternoon services on Rosh Hashanah. A congregation will meet at a river or stream and empty their pockets, usually consisting of breadcrumbs, into the water. This a symbol of emptying themselves of sin. Tashlich is based on Micah 7:19, which says, "He will again have compassion on us, And will subdue our iniquities. You will cast all our sins Into the depths of the sea."

Foods eaten on Rosh Hashanah are festive. Fruits and honeycakes are served. Apples and honey are also a traditional food enjoyed as a way of ushering in the New Year, a hopeful time where people desire the sweetness of life in the coming days. The most common greeting during the Jewish New Year season is, *"L'shanah tovah tikatevu,"* which means, "May your name be inscribed in the Book of Life."

Growing up in St. Petersburg, Florida, I attended a Reform synagogue. Reform Judaism is a liberal branch of Judaism. As a youth I attended services on Rosh Hashanah with my family and chimed in greeting people with, "May your name be inscribed in the Book of Life," while at the same time never pondering its significance. Why was that? In my Hebrew school studies as a youth, we didn't speak much about the Book of Life. Reform and Conservative Judaism are modern expressions of Judaism and teach that the deceased continue to exist in the memories of the living. Only Orthodox Jews believe in a literal resurrection from the dead, and within the whole of Judaism, there is no uniform view of death and the afterlife. The sages speculate, but most Jewish people today are uncertain about life beyond the grave.

Where does the Book of Life come from? It's referred to several places in the Hebrew scriptures, the Old Testament. Moses referred to the Book of Life in Exodus 32. Daniel 12 mentions it. David wrote in Psalm 69:28 about his enemies, "Let them be blotted out of the book of the living, And not be written with the righteous." As believers in Jesus Christ, we understand that same Book of Life is where our names are inscribed. In Philippians 4:3, the Apostle Paul refers to the book, "And I urge you also, true companion, help these women who labored with me in the gospel, with Clement also, and the rest of my fellow workers, whose names are in the Book of Life." Additionally, there are six verses in the book of Revelation that refer to the Book of Life. Specifically, in Revelation 3:5 Jesus promised that the names of all believers will not be erased from the Book of Life.

In Judaism, being in right relationship with God so that one can be inscribed in the Book of Life is certainly important from a biblical perspective, especially during the fall feast season. People want to be in right standing before God so they can be "happy" and "prosperous." We who know Messiah Jesus know also that He is the giver of all good gifts, and the happiness and prosperity He provides transcend both circumstance and time!

Jesus came to bring abundant and eternal life! In John 11:25–26, He said, "... I am the resurrection and the life. He who believes in Me, though he may die, he shall live. And whoever lives and believes in Me shall never die. ..." Since we who know the Lord are inscribed in the Book of Life, the Great Commission mandates us to go and tell others how they can have their names inscribed in the Book of Life. How? Not by righteous works we have done, but rather by trusting in Jesus and the righteous work on the cross he has accomplished for us! This is the basis of a right relationship with the Lord, and we know the beginning of that right relationship begins with repentance.

The Hebrew word *Teshuvah*, which can mean "to turn" or "to return," conveys this idea of repentance. For the believer, this turning from our sinfulness and turning to the righteousness of God found in Jesus Christ through faith is the beginning of our walk with the Lord. For the Jewish community, this concept of repentance is central to the observance that begins at Rosh Hashanah and runs through the ten days of awe. So, Rosh Hashanah is all about repentance.

The Day of Atonement—Yom Kippur

After Rosh Hashanah, it's with repentant hearts that Jewish people approach Yom Kippur, the Day of Atonement. This is the most awesome day, the tenth day of Tishri in the seventh month. The Lord instituted the Day of Atonement in Leviticus 23:26–32:

> And the LORD spoke to Moses, saying: "Also the tenth day of this seventh month shall be the Day of Atonement. It shall be a holy convocation for you; you shall afflict your souls, and offer an offering made by fire to the LORD. And you shall do no work on that same day, for it is the Day of Atonement, to make atonement for you before the LORD your God. For any person who is not afflicted in soul on that same day shall be cut off from his people. And any person who does any work on that same day, that person I will destroy from among his people. You shall do no manner of work; it shall be a statute forever throughout your generations in all your dwellings. It shall be to you a sabbath of solemn rest, and you shall afflict your souls; on the ninth day of the month at evening, from evening to evening, you shall celebrate your sabbath."

The Talmud, the Jewish oral law, simply refers to Yom Kippur as "The Day." Jewish people fast all day and implore God for forgiveness. The Hebrew word *yom* means "day." The Hebrew word *kippur* means "atonement," which comes from the Hebrew word *kapper*, meaning "to cover." As we've discussed, forgiveness of sins in the Old Testament was through the sacrificial system of atonement God gave Israel on the altar. The "life for life" principle is the foundation of the sacrificial system, specifically blood sacrifice.

Leviticus 17:11 states, "… I have given it to you upon the altar to make atonement for your souls; for it is the blood that makes atonement for the soul." Blood is the symbol of life. The blood of bulls, lambs, and goats was to be sacrificed by the high priest. On Yom Kippur, special sacrifices were to be made by the high priest. In Leviticus 16, God describes how these sacrifices were to be offered. The high priest was to ceremonially cleanse himself, preparing to enter the Holy of Holies in the tabernacle. This was where the very presence of God dwelt. The high priest was to only enter the Holy of Holies one day a year, on Yom Kippur. First, he was to offer sacrifices on the alter and sprinkle blood on the mercy seat to atone for his sins. Then two male goats were to be chosen by lot. The priests were to slaughter one goat and sprinkle its blood on the mercy seat, trusting that God would accept the sacrifices as atonement for the people of Israel. The high point of the ritual was the ceremony involving the second goat, called the scapegoat, which is described in Leviticus 16:21–22, where the Lord said:

> Aaron shall lay both his hands on the head of the live goat, confess over it all the iniquities of the children of Israel, and all their transgressions, concerning all their sins, putting them on the head of the goat, and shall send it away into the wilderness by the hand of a suitable man. The goat shall bear on itself all their iniquities to an uninhabited land; and he shall release the goat in the wilderness.

We noted that the central theme of Rosh Hashanah is repentance.

The main theme of Yom Kippur, the Day of Atonement, is redemption. Redemption, meaning the price paid to purchase someone out of slavery, comes from the Hebrew word *padah*, which was accomplished through the sacrificial system God provided on the altar. The temple in Jerusalem was destroyed in A.D. 70, and in the years immediately following that event, the leaders of Judaism came up with a new way to obtain redemption, the forgiveness of sins, without the temple.

As noted, when we studied the gospel in the Old Testament, the solution—a magic formula for forgiveness which was developed by the rabbis, without the temple—is this: We are forgiven through prayer, repentance, and *mitzvot*, or good works—of which you'll find many passages in the Old Testament. The underlying idea is that atonement and forgiveness depend on whether a man's good deeds outweigh his bad deeds, but is that really the way to eternal redemption?

As a missionary to my Jewish people in New York City for six years (2003–2009), I often asked Jewish people how they are having their sins forgiven without a sacrifice. Some quoted the rabbis, but most simply didn't have an answer. In fact, I've never had an unbelieving Jewish person tell me they walked out of the temple on Yom Kippur having assurance of forgiveness, nor has any sincere unbelieving Jewish person ever told me he has assurance his name is written in the Book of Life.

As believers in Messiah Jesus, we can have absolute assurance our sins are forgiven. Hallelujah! How does one find atonement without a temple? In Hebrews 9, the writer called Messiah Jesus our High Priest, and about His sacrificial death he wrote, " Not with the blood of goats and calves, but with His own blood He entered the Most Holy Place once for all, having obtained eternal redemption"

(v. 12). We don't trust in our own good works, but rather in the finished work of Jesus Christ on the cross!

He offered Himself as our sacrifice for sin, and He conquered the power of both sin and death when He arose on the third day. And we affirm and echo the words of the Apostle Paul, who wrote in 1 Corinthians 15:55, "O Death, where is your sting? O Hades, where is your victory?" For those who believe in Jesus, forgiveness is found! On a deeper note, Old Testament sacrifice was good only for the covering of sins. The sacrifice of Jesus, our High Priest, cleanses us of all sin! Old Testament sacrifice was temporary. Each year, Yom Kippur was to be observed, but Jesus' sacrifice was a one-time atonement. Jesus is my atonement today and every day; and in every way He has done it all for us! Now that's something to rejoice about. And rejoicing is what the Feast of Tabernacles is all about!

The Feast of Tabernacles—Sukkot

We go back to Leviticus 23, where God instituted the last of the fall feasts, the Feast of Tabernacles:

> Then the LORD spoke to Moses, saying, "Speak to the children of Israel, saying: 'The fifteenth day of this seventh month shall be the Feast of Tabernacles for seven days to the LORD. ... Also on the fifteenth day of the seventh month, when you have gathered in the fruit of the land, you shall keep the feast of the LORD for seven days; on the first day there shall be a sabbath-rest, and on the eighth day a sabbath-rest. And you shall take for yourselves on the first day the fruit of beautiful trees, branches of palm trees, the boughs of leafy trees, and willows of the brook; and you shall rejoice before the LORD your God for seven days. You shall keep it as a feast to the

Lord for seven days in the year. It shall be a statute forever in your generations. You shall celebrate it in the seventh month. You shall dwell in booths for seven days. All who are native Israelites shall dwell in booths, that your generations may know that I made the children of Israel dwell in booths when I brought them out of the land of Egypt: I am the Lord your God.'"

—Leviticus 23:33–34, 39–43

As the sun goes down marking the end of the Day of Atonement, Jewish people begin to build the Sukkah booth, preparing to celebrate the Feast of Tabernacles. In biblical times this was a joyful celebration of the final fall harvest, a time of ingathering at Jerusalem. It was the last of three feasts (along with Passover and Pentecost) when God commanded all males to come to Jerusalem. The Feast of Tabernacles or Sukkot (*sukkot* is a Hebrew word meaning "hut" or "booth") also commemorates God's deliverance of His people from Egypt and their forty years of wilderness wandering, when they lived in tents. God's tabernacle was with them. Jewish observers remember and rejoice in God's faithfulness and in His provision through the wilderness experience, so they build booths, or *sukkahs* and live in them for seven days. Even today, many Jewish people build open-roofed, three-sided huts for this festival. We decorate them with tree boughs and autumn fruits to remind us of the harvest.

One significant tradition that developed following God's institution of Sukkot in Leviticus 23, which became very prominent in Jesus' day, was called the "water pouring ceremony." In it, the priests brought water from the pool of Siloam and poured it into the altar, praying for abundant rain that was needed for future harvests. Since Israel was an agrarian society at that time, rain was essential for survival, because if they didn't get rains, they didn't get harvests.

There was also a messianic significance to this ceremony, that looked toward the outpouring of the Holy Spirit on Israel and the nations, too. The rain represented the Holy Spirit, and the water drawing pointed to that day when, according to the prophet Joel, God would rain His Spirit upon the Israelites. It's no coincidence that as the Jewish people were thinking about God's provision of rain for the harvest, and as they were celebrating and rejoicing in God's presence in the symbol of water, Jesus chose this ceremony to stand up and speak these words in John 7:37–38, "... If anyone is thirsty, let him come to Me and drink. He who believes in Me, as the Scripture has said, out of his heart will flow rivers of living water." We see Jesus using this symbol of water, something that Jewish people could see and understand, and applying it to His own life and ministry!

Sukkot, or the Feast of Tabernacles, also connects the dots between the temporal and eternal, as the Lord tabernacles with us through the person of the Holy Spirit. As we know, believers in Jesus are temples of the Holy Spirit, but the Bible also teaches us that sometime soon when the Lord returns, we as His church, the body of Messiah, will celebrate Sukkot for all eternity. As John wrote in Revelation 21:3–4:

> And I heard a loud voice from heaven saying, "Behold, the tabernacle of God is with men, and He will dwell with them, and they shall be His people. God Himself will be with them and be their God. And God will wipe away every tear from their eyes; there shall be no more death, nor sorrow, nor crying. There shall be no more pain, for the former things have passed away."

In that day, the whole world will become the Sukkah booth of God, and He will reign for all eternity. That will be a day of great rejoicing for all who know the love of Christ—both Jew and gentile alike! You and I, as believers in Jesus Christ, we also need to remember God's faithfulness and provision and rejoice in His goodness to us. So, as believers in Jesus Christ, the progression of the fall feasts of Israel is also a picture of our faith journey—repentance from our sin, redemption found in Jesus, and rejoicing in our salvation.

So concludes our brief but beautiful tour through the feasts of Israel—all fulfilled in our Lord Jesus, our Great God! Hallelujah!

Chapter 9 Study Guide

1. In order of observance, what are the fall feasts of Israel?
2. Why is the seventh month on the Hebrew calendar, Tishri, known as the "sacred month?"
3. In a word, how are each of the fall feasts described thematically?
4. Briefly describe the Feast of Trumpets (Rosh Hasahanah), then describe what occurs during the ten-day period between the Feast of Trumpets and Yom Kippur, the Day of Atonement.
5. What does the Hebrew word *teshuvah* mean?
6. Describe the ceremony of the "scapegoat" on Yom Kippur, the Day of Atonement, in Leviticus 16:21–22. How does this relate to the sacrifice of Christ, if at all?
7. According to Hebrews 9:12, what does the blood of Christ accomplish for the believer?
8. What did the Feast of Tabernacles (Sukkot) commemorate? What were the Israelites commanded to do during Sukkot that would help them remember and rejoice?
9. What was the messianic significance of the water pouring ceremony, a tradition surrounding the Feast of Tabernacles at the time of Christ? How did Jesus utilize this ceremony in teaching about Himself at the feast in John 7?
10. According to Revelation 21:3–4, what is the connection between the Feast of Tabernacles, the Christian, and the Lord?

Chapter 10

Messianic Prophecy: The Truth Is Out There!

If given the option to know what your future holds, would you do it? According to a recent study, most people wouldn't. Given the chance to see into the future, most people would rather not know what life has in store for them, even if they think those events could make them happy, according to recent research published by the American Psychological Association (APA).

In a 2017 study, the APA drew data from two nationally representative studies involving two thousand adults in Germany and Spain and found that 85 to 90 percent of people would not want to know about negative events in the future, and 40 to 70 percent felt the same about future positive events. In fact, only one percent of survey recipients consistently wanted to know about the future, according to the study, which was published in the journal *Psychological Review*.

The lead study author said in a news release. "Not wanting to know appears counterintuitive and may raise eyebrows, but deliberate ignorance, as we've shown here, doesn't just exist; it is a widespread state of mind."[12]

No doubt, there are limitations to this kind of study, because the

---

12. https://www.apa.org/news/press/releases/2017/02/know-future-

"future" can mean different things. For example, there is a "circumstantial" future of events in one's life, of which none of us can be sure, and there is an "ultimate future," the future that lies beyond the grave. As one popular TV show in the 1990s once quipped, "The truth is out there!" Regarding the veracity of messianic prophecy—indeed it is! Undoubtedly, due to the powerful statistics regarding death, this afterlife future is perhaps the one people most want to avoid facing, unless they have a saving relationship with the One who overcame the grave, namely Jesus!

We, as God's people, cannot only face, but embrace, our ultimate future with hope and joy because of the person and work of Jesus. Additionally, the Bible, the book of the future, gives us confidence that we can entrust our destiny wholly to the Alpha and Omega, the one who has promised us eternal life! To be sure, one of the dynamic aspects of the testimony of God's Word that should also grant God's people confidence is messianic prophecy.

What is messianic prophecy? It is the Bible's predictions about Jesus written in the Old Testament centuries before He was born. Why study messianic prophecy? It will strengthen your faith in the scriptures and help you connect biblical dots. Messianic prophecy also serves to help validate the claims of the Bible and is a credible witness for Jesus!

"All Scripture is given by inspiration of God ..." (2 Timothy 3:16), including Bible prophecy, and considering that more than twenty-five percent of the Bible is fulfilled, or yet to be fulfilled, prophecy, it is good to study it.

Why is so much of the Bible dedicated to prophecy? There are many reasons, but ultimately, for the sake of a gospel witness, it is to direct the attention of humanity to Jesus Christ. "... For the testimony of Jesus is the spirit of prophecy" (Revelation 19:10). The central tenet of both Old Testament prophecy and New Testament teaching is the gospel of Jesus!

Fulfilled prophecies lend unprecedented credibility to the Bible's claim to be the Word of God, and the messianic prophecies fulfilled by the birth, ministry, crucifixion, resurrection, and ascension of Jesus authenticate His claim to be the one true Christ. In essence, Bible prophecy is the most powerful witness to the divinity of Christ.

Messianic prophecy provides dynamic testimony supporting the veracity of God's Word and our future hope found in Jesus. If we study just seven specific prophecies that were later fulfilled in the person of Jesus Christ, we'll be amazed! It's impossible on a human level—yet with God, all things are possible! According to "conservative" estimates, here are the odds of Jesus fulfilling only seven prophecies:

» Jesus would be a descendant of David (1 in 10,000);
» Jesus would be born in Bethlehem (1 in 100,000);
» Jesus would be a miracle worker (1 in 100,000);
» Jesus would present Himself as King riding on a donkey (1 in 1,000,000);
» Jesus would be betrayed by a friend for thirty pieces of silver (1 in 1,000,000);
» Jesus would be crucified (1 in 1,000,000); and
» Jesus would first present Himself as King 173,880 days from the decree of Artaxerxes to rebuild Jerusalem (1 in 1,000,000).

The total probability (without God) of all of these prophecies being fulfilled by the same person is 10^{38}, which in numeral terms is 1 chance in 100 billion, billion, billion, billion![13]

---

13. https://www.bibletimelines.net/articles/is-jesus-really-the-messiah

Powerful indeed! In our brief survey, I'll provide just a small sample of messianic prophecies in the Old Testament and their fulfillment in the New Testament. We'll then examine and unpack three specific prophecies, unfolding the compelling back stories behind each, that your faith would be strengthened, and you would be emboldened with increased confidence to witness using this amazing biblical tool!

A Condensed Messianic Prophecy List

First, here's just a small sampling of forty-four messianic prophecies to wet your biblical appetite. I trust this starting point will encourage you to dig into the Word of God on your own and grow in your knowledge of Him.

Here are some major messianic prophecies and their fulfillment in the New Testament:

44 Prophecies Jesus Christ Fulfilled[14]

	Prophecies About Jesus	**Old Testament Scripture**	**New Testament Fulfillment**
1	Messiah would be born of a woman.	Genesis 3:15	Matthew 1:20 Galatians 4:4
2	Messiah would be born in *Bethlehem*.	Micah 5:2	Matthew 2:1 Luke 2:4–6
3	Messiah would be born of a virgin.	Isaiah 7:14	Matthew 1:22–23 Luke 1:26–31

---

14. https://parish.rcdow.org.uk/swisscottage/wp-content/uploads/sites/52/2014/11/44-Prophecies-Jesus-Christ-Fulfilled.pdf

	Prophecies About Jesus	**Old Testament Scripture**	**New Testament Fulfillment**
4	Messiah would come from the line of *Abraham*.	Genesis 12:3 Genesis 22:18	Matthew 1:1 Romans 9:5
5	Messiah would be a descendant of *Isaac*.	Genesis 17:19 Genesis 21:12	Luke 3:34
6	Messiah woild be a descendant of *Jacob*.	Numbers 24:17	Matthew 1:2
7	Messiah wold come from the tribe of Judah.	Genesis 49:10	Luke 3:33 Hebrews 7:14
8	Messiah would be heir to *King David's* throne.	2 Samuel 7:12–13 Isaiah 9:7	Luke 1:32–33 Romans 1:3
9	Messiah's throne will be anointed and eternal.	Psalm 45:6–7 Daniel 2:44	Luke 1:33 Hebrews 1:8–12
10	Messiah would be called *Immanuel*.	Isaiah 7:14	Matthew 1:23
11	Messiah would spend a season in Egypt.	Hosea 11:1	Matthew 2:14–15
12	Messiah would be born as human male and be divine.	Isaiah 9:6	John 1:1, 14
13	A messenger would prepare the way for Messiah.	Isaiah 40:3–5	Luke 3:3–6
14	Messiah would be rejected by his own people.	Psalm 69:8 Isaiah 53:3	John 1:11 John 7:5
15	Messiah would be a prophet.	Deuteronomy 18:15	Acts 3:20–22

	Prophecies About Jesus	**Old Testament Scripture**	**New Testament Fulfillment**
16	Messiah would be preceded by *Elijah*.	Malachi 4:5–6	Matthew 11:13–14
17	Messiah would be declared the Son of God.	Psalm 2:7	Matthew 3:16–17
18	Messiah would be called a Nazarene.	Isaiah 11:1	Matthew 2:23
19	Messiah would bring light to Galilee.	Isaiah 9:1–2	Matthew 4:13–16
20	Messiah would speak in *parables*.	Psalm 78:2–4 Isaiah 6:9–10	Matthew 13:10–15, 34–35
21	Messiah would be sent to heal the brokenhearted.	Isaiah 61:1–2	Luke 4:18-19
22	Messiah would be a priest after the order of *Melchizedek*.	Psalm 110:4	Hebrews 5:5–6
23	Messiah would be called King.	Psalm 2:6 Zecharah 9:9	Matthew 27:37 Matthew 21:1–11
24	Messiah would be praised by *little children*.	Psalm 8:2	Matthew 21:16
25	Messiah would be betrayed.	Psalm 41:9 Zechariah 11:12–13	Luke 22:47–48 Matthew 26:14–16
26	Messiah's price money would be used to buy a potter's field.	Zechariah 11:12–13	Matthew 27:9–10
27	Messiah would be falsely accused.	Psalm 35:11	Mark 14:57–58
28	Messiah would be silent before his accusers.	Isaiah 53:7	Mark 14:4–5

	Prophecies About Jesus	**Old Testament Scripture**	**New Testament Fulfillment**
29	Messiah would be spat upon and struck.	Isaiah 50:6	Matthew 26:67
30	Messiah would be hated without cause.	Psalm 35:19 Psalm 69:4	John 15:24–25
31	Messiah would be *crucified* with criminals.	Isaiah 53:12	Matthew 27:38 Mark 15:27–28
32	Messiah would be given vinegar to drink.	Psalm 69:21	Matthew 27:34 John 19:28–30
33	Messiah's hands and feet would be pierced.	Psalm 22:16 Zechariah 12:10	John 20:25–27
34	Messiah would be mocked and ridiculed.	Psalm 22:7–8	Luke 23:35
35	Soldiers woule gamble for Messiah's garments.	Psalm 22:18	Luke 23:34 Matthew 27:35–36
36	Messiah's bones would not be broken.	Exodus 12:46 Psalm 34:20	John 19:33–36
37	Messiah would be forsaken by God.	Psalm 22:1	Matthew 27:46
38	Messiah would pray for His enemies.	Psalm 109:4	Luke 23:34
39	Soldiers would pierce Messiah's side.	Zechariah 12:10	John 19:34
40	Messiah would be buried with the rich.	Isaiah 53:9	Matthew 27:57–60
41	Messiah would *resurrect* from the dead.	Psalm 16:10 Psalm 49:15	Matthew 28:2–7 Acts 2:22–32
42	Messiah would ascend to heaven.	Psalm 24:7–10	Mark 16:19 Luke 24:51

	Prophecies About Jesus	Old Testament Scripture	New Testament Fulfillment
43	Messiah would be seated at God's right hand.	Psalm 68:18 Psalm 110:1	Matthew 22:44
44	Messiah would be a *sacrifice* for sin.	Isaiah 53:5–12	Romans 5:6–8

Three Compelling Backstories!

It's one thing to connect Old Testament prophecy with New Testament fulfillment, but our degree of understanding and encouragement will be enhanced as we also unpack, with some detail, just a few of the major prophecies concerning our Lord Jesus. Keep in mind that we could do an in-depth survey of many more messianic prophecies. Due to the limits of our survey, we're only feasting on a few bites, but—oh, how delicious these bites!

Messiah would be born in Bethlehem. On the surface, this prophecy about the birthplace of Jesus is straightforward. Upon further review concerning the timing and location of His birth, along with the circumstances surrounding His birth, there is certainly more than meets the eye.

Micah 5:2 established the prophecy, ""But you, Bethlehem Ephrathah, though you are little among the thousands of Judah, Yet out of you shall come forth to Me The One to be Ruler in Israel, Whose goings forth are from of old, From everlasting."

Note in verse 2 that the "goings forth" of this "Ruler in Israel" are "from of old, From **everlasting**." The Hebrew word for everlasting in this verse is *olam*, which may mean a long duration, forever, perpetual, or in this case, everlasting. In the Old Testament, "everlasting" and "forever" are far and away the most common uses of the word *olam*. There is only one throne that is everlasting—that is the Throne of God! Therefore, the King of Kings, Jesus, will ultimately sit on this throne.

Roughly eight centuries later, the prophecy is fulfilled in Matthew 2:1, where the scripture simply declares, "Now after Jesus was born in Bethlehem of Judea in the days of Herod the king, behold, wise men from the East came to Jerusalem."

Additionally, Luke 2:1–5 gives us a glimpse into the surrounding circumstances, namely a census, which dictated that Joseph and Mary, residents of Nazareth, had to make a trek to Bethlehem:

> And it came to pass in those days that a decree went out from Caesar Augustus that all the world should be registered. This census first took place while Quirinius was governing Syria. So all went to be registered, everyone to his own city. Joseph also went up from Galilee, out of the city of Nazareth, into Judea, to the city of David, which is called Bethlehem, because he was of the house and lineage of David, to be registered with Mary, his betrothed wife, who was with child.

It was a ninety-mile trek from Nazareth to Bethlehem (the town of Joseph's ancestors). People could travel twenty miles or so per day! Some scholars say Joseph and Mary may have only traveled around ten miles per day due to her pregnancy! However long it took, it was a number of days in transit!

The incredible reality is that they made it to Bethlehem at just the right time for the Son of God to be born. Mary could have given birth sometime prior to their arrival in Bethlehem, or Jesus could have been born anytime after they left Bethlehem. Yet God's timing is perfect. He's never late nor early, but has made "… everything beautiful in its time ..." (Ecclesiastes 3:11). As the Apostle Paul affirmed in Galatians 4:4, "But when the fullness of the time had come, God sent forth His Son, born of a woman. ..."

There's more! Bethlehem in Hebrew is *Beth*, meaning "house," combined with the Hebrew word *lechem*, meaning "bread." So, Bethlehem literally means "house of bread." If you remember, in John 6:35 Jesus referred to Himself as "the bread of life." In other words, the "bread of life"—Jesus—was born in the "house of bread"—Bethlehem. Hallelujah!

Messiah would be a descendant of Abraham and of Jacob. Genealogies are sometimes avoided or overlooked, because there are many lists in the Bible. "So and so" begat "so and so" who begat "so and so." We get it. Genealogies may be difficult to grasp and understand, yet they can be or great importance. There's no more important genealogy than that of the Son of God, Jesus.

In the book of Genesis, God promised Abraham that the Messiah would be his descendant. As we studied earlier in our introduction of the Abrahamic Covenant, the Lord told Abraham in Genesis 12:3, "... in you all the families of the earth shall be blessed," while reaffirming the promise to Abraham in Genesis 22:18 declaring, "In your seed all the nations of the earth shall be blessed, because you have obeyed My voice."

In Numbers 24:17 the Lord also stated that the Messiah would be a descendant of Jacob, "I see Him, but not now; I behold Him, but not near; A Star shall come out of Jacob; A Scepter shall rise out of Israel. ..." The "scepter" is important and connected also to Genesis 49:10, which says, "The scepter shall not depart from Judah, Nor a lawgiver from between his feet, Until Shiloh comes; And to Him shall be the obedience of the people."

The word "scepter" means "rod" or "staff," and usually indicates authority. Scepter is also used to symbolize God's rule, as in Psalm 45:6: "Your throne, O God, is forever and ever; A scepter of righteousness is the scepter of Your kingdom."

In addition, while Shiloh is a geographical location in Israel, the usage in Psalm 49:10 refers specifically to the Messiah!

With that background, we come to the fulfillment of this prophecy at the very beginning of Matthew's gospel: "The book of the genealogy of Jesus Christ, the Son of David, the Son of Abraham: Abraham begot Isaac, Isaac begot Jacob, and Jacob begot Judah and his brothers" (Matthew 1:1–2).

Regarding fulfillment of the prophecy, all the families of the Earth have certainly been blessed by Messiah Jesus. As Isaiah 42:6 proclaims, "… I will also give You as a light to the Gentiles [nations]. …" In the not-so-distant future, at the Second Coming of Christ, Jesus will rule and reign with the scepter, "that at the name of Jesus every knee should bow, of those in heaven, and of those on earth, and of those under the earth, and that every tongue should confess that Jesus Christ is Lord, to the glory of God the Father" (Philippians 2:10–11).

Messiah would be a prophet. Moses is Judaism's greatest prophet. During one of his last speeches to his people Israel, Moses said in Deuteronomy 18:15, "The Lord your God will raise up for you a Prophet like me from your midst, from your brethren. Him you shall hear."

Jesus would be like Moses in many ways. For example, Moses was both a prophet and a lawgiver, as was Jesus. In His time on Earth, Jesus was widely recognized as a prophet who spoke the Word of God (Matthew 21:46), and He gave commandments for His followers (John 13:34; 15:12, 17; Galatians 6:2).

Moses spent forty years as a shepherd (Exodus 3:1), and Jesus is called the Good Shepherd (John 10:11, 14). Moses and Jesus also were alike in that they both led God's people out of captivity, and Moses was like Jesus in that he performed miracles—not all prophets did.

When John the Baptist began his public ministry, preaching repentance and preparing the way of the Lord in the first century, some people wondered if he was the prophet to whom Moses referred. That's why in John 1 Jewish people interrogated John regarding his identity, questioning him about who he was and why he was baptizing. Their question, "… Are you the Prophet? …" (John 1:21) demonstrated they were looking for the fulfillment of Moses' prophecy. John answered "No" and pointed them to the One who was: "… I baptize with water, but there stands One among you whom you do not know. It is He who, coming after me, is preferred before me, whose sandal strap I am not worthy to loose" (John 1:26–27).

When Jesus began His public ministry, He was not only a prophet like Moses, fulfilling Deuteronomy 18:15, He was also a prophet greater than Moses, as Hebrews 3:1–3 reveals,

> Therefore, holy brethren, partakers of the heavenly calling, consider the Apostle and High Priest of our confession, Christ Jesus, who was faithful to Him who appointed Him, as Moses also was faithful in all His house. For this One has been counted worthy of more glory than Moses, inasmuch as He who built the house has more honor than the house.

While Peter was preaching in Solomon's portico in Acts 3, he testified that Jesus is the prophet to whom Moses referred, while also noting Jesus' connection to the Abrahamic Covenant:

"Repent therefore and be converted, that your sins may be blotted out, so that times of refreshing may come from the presence of the Lord, and that He may send Jesus Christ, who was preached to you before, whom heaven must receive until the times of restoration of all things, which God has spoken by the mouth of all His holy prophets since the world began. **For Moses truly said to the fathers, 'The Lord your God will raise up for you a Prophet like me from your brethren. Him you shall hear in all things, whatever He says to you.** And it shall be that every soul who will not hear that Prophet shall be utterly destroyed from among the people.' Yes, and all the prophets, from Samuel and those who follow, as many as have spoken, have also foretold these days. You are sons of the prophets, and of the covenant which God made with our fathers, saying to Abraham, 'And in your seed all the families of the earth shall be blessed.' To you first, God, having raised up His Servant Jesus, sent Him to bless you, in turning away every one of you from your iniquities."

—Acts 3:19–26

Parting Shots on Messianic Prophecy

There's so much more we could investigate, as massive volumes have been written on the topic of messianic prophecy. For example, David prophesied that Messiah's hands and feet would be pierced, when he wrote in Psalm 22:16, "For dogs have surrounded Me; The congregation of the wicked has enclosed Me. They pierced My hands and My feet." When David penned those words some ten centuries before Christ, crucifixion had not yet even been invented! It would be about four hundred years after David wrote Psalm 22, when the Persians would invent that horrific form of execution. It would be the Romans who perfected crucifixion.

We didn't mention prophecies concerning the Second Coming of Christ, but be encouraged! If Jesus fulfilled every prophecy regarding His first coming, we can be sure He will fulfill every prophecy concerning His Second Coming. As the Apostle Paul exclaimed in 2 Corinthians 1:20, "For all the promises of God in Him are Yes, and in Him Amen, to the glory of God through us."

As we conclude our brief survey on messianic prophecy, may it not only encourage and strengthen our faith, may we also see it as a powerful evangelistic tool. While we understand unbelievers may want to avoid discussing an uncertain future, messianic prophecy is certainly a powerful tool to have in our evangelistic toolbox. "Future" evangelism is good news about the future, and everyone must face the reality of death, as the statistics are impressive. The good news is that Jesus conquered sin and death through His sacrifice on the cross and resurrection three days later. For the one who trusts in Him, there is a future filled with hope. Because He lives, we who know Him shall also live. As he declared in John 11:25–26, "… I am the resurrection and the life. He who believes in Me, though he may die, he shall live. And whoever lives and believes in Me shall never die. Do you believe this?"

May we who know Jesus share with others this singular hope in the One who holds the future in His hands!

Chapter 10 Study Guide

1. What is messianic prophecy?
2. Why should we study messianic prophecy?
3. How much of the Bible is either fulfilled, or to be fulfilled, prophecy?
4. What prophecies we've discussed or listed have most strengthened your faith? Why?
5. Regarding the Micah 5:2 prophecy that the Messiah was to be born in Bethlehem, what aspect of its fulfillment evokes awe and wonder in you, and why?
6. Regarding the prophecy that the Messiah was to be a descendant of Abraham and of Jacob, how do you personally feel about studying genealogies? How does the unpacking of this one change, if at all, your perspective on biblical genealogies?
7. Regarding the prophecy that the Messiah would be a prophet like Moses, how was Jesus like Moses?
8. According to Hebrews 3:1–3, how was Jesus like Moses, and how was he different from Moses?
9. How does Peter utilize the prophecy that the Messiah would be a prophet like Moses as he preached in Acts 3:19–26?
10. How might you utilize messianic prophecy in your witness to others?

Chapter 11

The Trinity in the Old Testament

The Rorschach test is a psychological test in which subjects' perceptions of inkblots are recorded and then analyzed using psychological interpretation, complex algorithms, or both. Some psychologists use this test to examine a person's personality characteristics and emotional functioning. Made famous by Swiss psychologist Hermann Rorschach, who created his first inkblot in 1921, these series of inkblot images are perceived in different ways by different people![15]

We have all gazed upon inkblot images and perceived different things. Some people call these images optical illusions, but there is no denying that with inkblots, you and I can look at the same one and see different things. In one sense, "hidden in plain sight" may also describe both inkblots and other optical illusions that we gaze upon. The interesting thing is that if we were to stare at the same image, what I see and what you see may both be present. We're just gazing at the image through a different perceptive prism.

As we continue our study of Jewish roots, we come to the fascinating topic of the Trinity in the Old Testament. As we stop on our

---
15. https://en.wikipedia.org/wiki/Rorschach_test

biblical survey, you may be surprised to see some scriptures in a different light—through a different prism—a broader prism.

As we touch upon highlights, please grant me grace as the material presented in this chapter will be a bit more "technical" from a biblical perspective than I've presented so far. Yet I trust you'll be edified and hopefully see some things in the Word of God that you haven't seen before, that have always been present—kind of like a biblical inkblot.

God Is a plurality!

God is a multi-faceted multi-dimensional being! What do I mean by that? Well, whatever our paradigm of God is, He is bigger! And whatever our understanding of God is, He is more complex.

You've perhaps heard it said that the Bible doesn't tell us everything there is to know. It simply tells us everything we need to know. As God reveals Himself to us in the Holy Scriptures, we are introduced to a being much bigger and more complicated being than we could even begin to fathom. With that said, the first words from God's Word are illustrative.

As world-class biblical scholar Arnold Fruchtenbaum, a Jewish believer in Jesus, states in his enlightening article entitled, *Jewishness and the Trinity*, "God is a plurality. It is generally agreed that the Hebrew word *Elohim* is a plural noun having the masculine plural ending "im." The very word *Elohim* is used of the true God in Genesis 1:1, "In the beginning God created the heavens and the earth."[16]

Regarding plurality, Fruchtenbaum adds that in Hebrew grammar, the Lord will often refer to Himself using the plural pronoun.

16/ *Jewishness & the Trinity* by Dr. Arnold Fruchtenbaum @jewsforjesus.org/publications/issues/1_8/jewish

For example, Genesis 1:26 states, "... Then God (Elohim) said, "Let Us make man in Our image, according to Our likeness. ..." Here the Lord would not have been referring to angels since man was created in the image of God, and not of angels. Other biblical examples where we see the use of the plural pronoun are:

- **Genesis 3:22:** "Then the Lord God [YHVH Elohim] said, 'Behold, the man has become like one of Us.'..."
- **Genesis 11:7:** "Come, let Us go down, and there confuse their language. ..."
- **Isaiah 6:8:** "Also I heard the voice of the Lord, saying, 'Whom shall I send, and who will go for Us?'..."

God—A Compound One!

The greatest confession of faith in Judaism, called the Shema (meaning "hear"), is the declaration I sang often growing up in the synagogue: **"Hear, O Israel: The Lord our God, the Lord is one!"** (Deuteronomy 6:4).

Fruchtenbaum provides continuing perspective on this compound "one":

> Deuteronomy 6:4, known as the Shema, has always been Israel's great confession. A glance through the Hebrew text where the word is used elsewhere can quickly show that the word echad does not mean an absolute "one," but a compound "one." For instance, in Genesis 1:5 the combination of evening and morning comprise one (echad) day. In Genesis 2:24 a man and a woman come together in marriage, and the two "shall become one [echad] flesh."[17]

---

17. Ibid.

Is God a Triune God? Yes!

If the Old Testament actually points to a plurality, then we might ask, "How many personalities exist in the Godhead?" As we'll discover, there are clearly three distinct personalities in the Jewish scriptures that are ever considered divine.

The Father. In the Old Testament there are numerous places where you'll read the word "LORD"—this is considered in Judaism to be "Lord YHVH." This is a reference to the Father. For example, Genesis 4:1–4 reads:

> Now Adam knew Eve his wife, and she conceived and bore Cain, and said, "I have acquired a man from the LORD." Then she bore again, this time his brother Abel. Now Abel was a keeper of sheep, but Cain was a tiller of the ground. And in the process of time it came to pass that Cain brought an offering of the fruit of the ground to the LORD. Abel also brought of the firstborn of his flock and of their fat. And the LORD respected Abel and his offering.

YHVH is called the **tetragrammaton** (meaning "four letters" in Greek); It's derived from the verb that means "to be" and is considered in Judaism to be a proper *name of the God of Israel* used in the *Hebrew Bible*. It's commonly pronounced "Yahweh," though *"Jehovah"* is used in many bibles. Orthodox Jews are forbidden to say or write the tetragrammaton in full. Traditionally in Judaism, the name is not pronounced but read as *"Adonai"* ("Master" or "Lord") during prayer, and referred to as *"HaShem"* ("The Name") at all other times.[18]

---

18. Ibid.

This reference to God, the Father, "LORD," (ALL CAPS IS THE KEY) is used well over five thousand times in the Jewish scriptures and is by far the most common name for God in the Old Testament.

As a missionary to my Jewish people in New York City from 2003 to 2009, I had a gospel witness to a few Orthodox Jewish men. While the origin of the prohibition against stating God's name is unclear, many Orthodox Jewish people will not utter His proper name, "God." Instead, they will simply refer to God as "the Name." At one time in New York City, I regularly met with an Orthodox Jewish man named Isaac to share the truth claims of Jesus to be the Messiah. Usually upon our initial salutations, Isaac would shake my hand and endearingly exclaim, *"Baruch HaShem"*—meaning "Blessed be the Name." This was one of the ways he expressed praise without uttering "God."

The Son. In the Hebrew scriptures, the Old Testament, a second personality is referred to either as "Son" or "the Angel of the Lord."

As an example, Daniel 7:13 states, "I was watching in the night visions, And behold, One like the Son of Man, Coming with the clouds of heaven! He came to the Ancient of Days, And they brought Him near before Him." Jesus often referred to Himself as the "Son of Man." In fact, the Lord referred to Himself as the "Son of Man" more often than any other self-designation in the gospels. For example, in Matthew 12:8, Jesus said, "For the Son of Man is Lord even of the Sabbath." In Mark 10:45, He announced, "For even the Son of Man did not come to be served, but to serve, and to give His life a ransom for many."

Note the reference to the "Son" in Proverbs 30:4—this time in a specific question about the Son of God, "Who has ascended into heaven, or descended? Who has gathered the wind in His fists? Who has bound the waters in a garment? Who has established all the ends of the earth? What is His name, and what is His Son's name, If you know?" I personally love this verse and have used it on occasion in witnessing encounters with my Jewish people, because as you might imagine, the "Son of God" has no place in Judaism!

In Isaiah 9:6–7, we find a powerful passage that reveals a son who is characterized by divinity:

> For unto us a Child is born, Unto us a Son is given; And the government will be upon His shoulder. And His name will be called Wonderful, Counselor, Mighty God, Everlasting Father, Prince of Peace. Of the increase of His government and peace There will be no end, Upon the throne of David and over His kingdom, To order it and establish it with judgment and justice From that time forward, even forever. The zeal of the Lord of hosts will perform this.

This compelling prophecy about Messiah contains several elements revealing His deity. First of all, this child who is born, this Son who is given, will be called "Mighty God" and "Everlasting Father." That's pretty clear. A child, a son, who is given these monikers? Sounds compelling, doesn't it?

Additionally, note that His government will be eternal, as verse 7 declares, "Of the increase of His government and peace There will be no end, Upon the throne of David and over His kingdom, To order it and establish it with judgment and justice From that time forward, even forever. ..." There is only one government that is eternal—God's—and the One Who will sit on the throne of David forever? That would be the King of Kings, Jesus, the Messiah (Revelation 17:14, 19:16)!

The exact identity of the "Angel of the Lord" in the Old Testament is not given, although many Bible scholars and theologians will describe His appearance as theophanies, or pre-incarnate manifestations of Jesus Christ. This individual is always seen as unique and distinct from all other angels. There are several places where He is referred to as both the "Angel of the LORD" and the "LORD" Himself. In the case of Manoah and his wife, the parents of Samson, which we'll soon see, they will testify from their perspective as to the exact identity of the Angel of the Lord.

One Bible commentator puts it well:

> The angel of the Lord speaks as God, identifies Himself with God, and exercises the responsibilities of God (Genesis 16:7–12; 21:17–18; 22:11–18; Exodus 3:2; Judges 2:1–4; 5:23; 6:11–24; 13:3–22; 2 Samuel 24:16; Zechariah 1:12; 3:1; 12:8). In several of these appearances, those who saw the angel of the Lord feared for their lives because they had "seen the Lord." Therefore, it is clear that in at least some instances, the angel of the Lord is a theophany, an appearance of God in physical form."[19]

In one example we find in Judges 13, Manoah and his wife, the parents of Samson, had an encounter with the Angel of the Lord. In Judges 13:2–3 the Angel of the Lord appeared to the wife of Manoah:

> Now there was a certain man from Zorah, of the family of the Danites, whose name was Manoah; and his wife was barren and had no children. And the Angel of the LORD appeared to the woman and said to her, "Indeed now, you are barren and have borne no children, but you shall conceive and bear a son."

In Judges 13:6–7 the woman described this angel to her husband Manoah:

---

19. https://www.gotquestions.org/angel-of-the-Lord.html

> So the woman came and told her husband, saying, "A Man of God came to me, and His countenance was like the countenance of the Angel of God, very awesome; but I did not ask Him where He was from, and He did not tell me His name. And He said to me, 'Behold, you shall conceive and bear a son. Now drink no wine or similar drink, nor eat anything unclean, for the child shall be a Nazirite to God from the womb to the day of his death.'"

Later in the dramatic conclusion to the narrative, Manoah and his wife came to a striking conclusion about the true identity of this Angel of the Lord:

> Then Manoah said to the Angel of the Lord, "Please let us detain You, and we will prepare a young goat for You." And the Angel of the Lord said to Manoah, "Though you detain Me, I will not eat your food. But if you offer a burnt offering, you must offer it to the Lord." (For Manoah did not know He was the Angel of the Lord.) Then Manoah said to the Angel of the Lord, "What is Your name, that when Your words come to pass we may honor You?" And the Angel of the Lord said to him, "Why do you ask My name, seeing it is wonderful?" So Manoah took the young goat with the grain offering, and offered it upon the rock to the Lord. And He did a wondrous thing while Manoah and his wife looked on—it happened as the flame went up toward heaven from the altar—the Angel of the Lord ascended in the flame of the altar! When Manoah and his wife saw this, they fell on their faces to the ground. **When the Angel of the Lord appeared no more to Manoah and his wife, then Manoah knew that He was the Angel of the Lord. And Manoah said to his wife, "We shall surely die, because we have seen God!"**
>
> —Judges 13:15–22

The Holy Spirit. A third major personality of the Godhead revealed in the Old Testament is the Spirit of God, otherwise known in Hebrew as the *Ruach HaKadosh*, which we would render in English, "the Holy Spirit." *Ruach* is Hebrew for "wind," "breath," or "spirit." *Kadosh* means "holy," while the Hebrew word *Ha* means "the."

I would commend to you a word study of "spirit" in the Old Testament, as it will bless your understanding. There are a good number of references to the Holy Spirit in the Hebrew scriptures. For example, Genesis 1:1–2 states, "In the beginning God created the heavens and the earth. The earth was without form, and void; and darkness was on the face of the deep. And the **Spirit of God** was hovering over the face of the waters." What is the Spirit of God in verse 2? That is the *Ruach HaKadosh*.

As God was preparing to judge the earth through the great flood in Noah's time, He said in Genesis 6:3, "And the Lord said, **'My Spirit** shall not strive with man forever, for he is indeed flesh; yet his days shall be one hundred and twenty years.'"

In Numbers 11:16–17 note that God the Father made reference to God the Spirit, as the Lord empowered the "elders of Israel:"

> So the LORD said to Moses: "Gather to Me seventy men of the elders of Israel, whom you know to be the elders of the people and officers over them; bring them to the tabernacle of meeting, that they may stand there with you. Then I will come down and talk with you there. **I will take of the Spirit that is upon you and will put the same upon them;** and they shall bear the burden of the people with you, that you may not bear it yourself alone."

After committing adultery with Bathsheba and murdering her husband Uriah, David pleaded with the Lord not to take the Spirit from him, when he, in repentance, cried out in Psalm 51:11, "Do not cast me away from Your presence, And **do not take Your Holy Spirit from me."**

David also made reference to the *Ruach HaKadosh*, when he wrote in Psalm 139:7, **"Where can I go from Your Spirit?** Or where can I flee from Your presence?"

The Word of God states in Job 33:4, **"The Spirit of God has made me,** And the breath of the Almighty gives me life."

Finally, we see one last example of the *Ruach Hakadosh* in Isaiah 11:2, **"The Spirit of the Lord shall rest upon Him,** The Spirit of wisdom and understanding, The Spirit of counsel and might, The Spirit of knowledge and of the fear of the Lord."

An in-depth inquiry of the Holy Spirit in the entirety of scripture will clearly reveal that He cannot be a mere emanation because He contains all the characteristics of personality (intellect, emotion, and will) and is considered divine.

Father and Son

Psalm 2 is considered a "royal" psalm, as it contains royal imagery, or that pertaining to a king. In this case, that king would be a reference to the Messiah who takes His rightful place on the throne of David. Additionally, we find in this powerful psalm a picture of God the Father establishing the kingship of God, the Son on David's throne, which, as we discovered earlier, is eternal. We know there is only one throne that is eternal—God's throne.

Let's briefly unpack this incredible psalm that sheds light on Messiah's triumph and kingdom. In Psalm 2:1–3, note the nations raging against God and His Anointed:

> Why do the nations rage, And the people plot a vain thing? The kings of the earth set themselves, And the rulers take counsel together, **Against the Lord and against His Anointed,** saying, "Let us break Their bonds in pieces And cast away Their cords from us."

We see God the Father communicated as **"LORD"** in verse two, as we learned earlier. "His Anointed" is a reference to the Messiah. Remember, the term *Messiah* literally means "Anointed One."

In Psalm 2:4–9, we read of God's response to the conspiring and scheming of mankind:

> He who sits in the heavens shall laugh; The Lord shall hold them in derision. Then He shall speak to them in His wrath, And distress them in His deep displeasure: **"Yet I have set My King On My holy hill of Zion." "I will declare the decree: The Lord has said to Me, 'You are My Son, Today I have begotten You. Ask of Me, and I will give You The nations for Your inheritance, And the ends of the earth for Your possession.** You shall break them with a rod of iron; You shall dash them to pieces like a potter's vessel.'"

Once established as King in Zion, another name for Jerusalem, the installed King then recites the LORD's decree, by declaring in verse 7, "The LORD has said to Me, 'You are my Son, today I have begotten You.'…" This is the first place in the Hebrew scriptures referring to the Father/Son relationship within the Trinity! In addition, Psalm 2:7 is quoted in the New Testament with reference to the birth of Jesus (Hebrews 1:5–6).

As Psalm 2 concludes in verses 10–12, we highlight the command to "Kiss the Son" in verse 12,

"Now therefore, be wise, O kings; Be instructed, you judges of the earth. Serve the Lord with fear, And rejoice with trembling. **Kiss the Son,** lest He be angry, And you perish in the way, When His wrath is kindled but a little. Blessed are all those who put their trust in Him."

In its original context, the phrase "kiss the son" referred to an act of submission or obedience. The recipients of this psalm were to "kiss His Son" or submit to the Lord. In fact, other translations of the phrase include "submit to God's royal Son" and "do homage to the Son."

At least two examples of kissing as a symbol of submission are found elsewhere in the Old Testament. Samuel anointed Saul as king in 1 Samuel 10:1, "Then Samuel took a flask of oil and poured it on his head, and kissed him and said: 'Is it not because the Lord has anointed you commander over His inheritance?'" In 1 Kings 19:18, God told Elijah, "Yet I reserve seven thousand in Israel, all whose knees have not bowed down to Baal, and every mouth that has not kissed him." In both verses, kissing shows allegiance or submission.[20]

Praise the Lord for clearly communicating aspects of the Trinity and the Kingship of the Son, Messiah in Psalm 2—a powerful testimony indeed!

To tie up our thoughts on the Trinity in the Jewish scriptures, the perception of some people is that the nature of the God of the Old Testament is somehow different from the God of the New Testament. I hope our brief survey has helped dispel such a myth, for God is the same yesterday, today, and forever (Hebrews 13:8).

And as we've studied the Trinity in the Old Testament, I trust your faith has been strengthened and your understanding of God's

---

20   https://www.gotquestions.org/kiss-the-son.html

Word expanded as we've examined scriptures pointing to the God's triune nature.

To God be all the glory—Father, Son, and Spirit! Amen.

Chapter 11 Study Guide

1. Prior to reading this chapter, what was your understanding of the Trinity in the Old Testament?
2. Regarding "the Father" in the Old Testament, what is the rendering for God that is used most often in the Hebrew scriptures and refers to God, the Father?
3. As we learned, YHVH is called the *tetragrammaton* (meaning "four letters" in Greek). It's derived from the verb that means "to be" and is considered in Judaism to be a proper name of the God of Israel used in the Hebrew Bible. Why won't some Orthodox Jewish people utter the name "God?"
4. What other moniker is also ascribed to the Son of God in the Old Testament?
5. In Isaiah 9:6–7 what are some of the striking characteristics of this particular "son?" How might you utilize this verse in witnessing to people regarding the person of Jesus?
6. How do the words and actions of the "Angel of the Lord" make a compelling case that He is, in fact, God?
7. In the account of Manoah and his wife, the parents of Samson, in Judges 13:15–22, what do they conclude about the "Angel of the Lord" that they have encountered?
8. *Ruach HaKadosh*, is Hebrew for "The Holy Spirit." From our study break down the words *Ruach* and *Kadosh* into there individual meanings to enhance your understanding.
9. Use a concordance to do a brief word study of "spirit" in the Jewish scriptures. Note the different ways the Spirit impacts people.
10. In simple terms, did you learn anything new as a result of this brief study?

Chapter 12

New Testament Applications

Once while visiting an antique store, my wonderful wife Lori grabbed my attention and pointed out a large, framed picture to me—at least upon first glance it appeared to be a picture. Alas! Upon closer inspection it was actually a jigsaw puzzle with every piece in its proper place. It looked awesome. I can only imagine the satisfaction the person or persons who completed the project felt about their feat!

Jigsaw puzzles take time, patience, and some perseverance. Yet, what once were a large number of disconnected pieces that lacked meaning, become a cohesive unit which is clearly understandable—you see the complete image!

Such has been our endeavor as we've taken a journey down Redemption Road, seeking a deeper and clearer understanding of the gospel and the person and work of Jesus through our study of the Jewish roots of Christianity! You've made it this far, and I applaud you for your effort on the journey. I hope it's been edifying for you!

In this final chapter, we'll endeavor to complete our "jigsaw puzzle"—as we connect dots between the Old Testament and New Testament with the goal of more clearly seeing God's redemptive plan for mankind found in the person and work of our Messiah and Lord—Jesus.

We know that in order to better understand a text of scripture, we need to better understand the context in which it was written. Who? What? When? Where? Why? The answers to these and other questions will amplify our understanding of scripture as we study.

What is the overall context for better understanding the New Testament text? Yes, it's the Old Testament! Remember, together they are the whole counsel of God. The whole of scripture is the revelation of God given to mankind, and the common thread running throughout is the thread of redemption, as we have noted.

In this chapter, we'll examine the feasts of Israel in light of the ministry of Christ in the gospels. In addition, we'll also see how to maximize New Testament study by identifying "tells" in the text, clues that will prompt us to cross reference Old Testament passages referred to in the New Testament account.

Jesus and the Feasts of Israel in the New Testament

After all our inquiry into God's Word, it may surprise you to know that there are many places in the gospel accounts where the setting of Jesus' teaching was a Jewish feast. Why would Jesus be in Jerusalem during one of these feasts? Well, to reach His Jewish people, of course! As He declared in Matthew 15:24, "… I was not sent except to the lost sheep of the house of Israel." These important times in the religious life of the Jewish people were also settings for important teachings given by the Messiah.

Jesus and Passover. The "Passion Week" is in the context of Passover. Jesus was crucified on Passover and resurrected on Firstfruits. The passages below all take place during the beginning of the Passion Week, beginning at the "triumphal entry" on Palm Sunday" and running through Passover and Firstfruits.

- » Matthew 21:1–17; Matthew 26:17–28:10
- » Mark 11:1–10; Mark 14:12–16:11
- » Luke 19:28–40; Luke 22:1–24:12
- » John 12:12–19; John 13:1–20:18

Remember, in John 1:29 John the Baptist looked at Y'shua (Jesus), and declared, "Behold! The Lamb of God who takes away the sin of the world!" Jesus was to offer Himself as the sacrifice for sin. Just as the Passover lambs were slain in remembrance of the deliverance from physical bondage in Egypt, so Jesus, the Lamb of God, was slain in order to deliver people out of spiritual bondage to sin.

One striking detail about the context of Jesus' teaching during Passover is found in the Gospel of John. Note in John 13 that the last supper was actually a Passover Seder meal, and Jesus' teaching at that moment, commonly known as the "upper room discourse," occurred at the same time. The remainder of this section of scripture through John 20:18 took place during Passover. The context of John 13:1–20:18, which is Passover, is roughly thirty percent of the entire gospel account! That's significant, as the connections are striking between Passover and the Lamb of God, who was to be the sacrifice for sin!

Jesus and the Feast of Tabernacles. In John 7 and 8, Jesus was teaching in the context of the Feast of Tabernacles. As we learned earlier, Passover, the Feast of Tabernacles, and Pentecost (also known as Shavuot) were the three feasts Jewish men were commanded to observe in Jerusalem (Deuteronomy 16:16).

John 7:1–2 states, "After these things Jesus walked in Galilee; for

He did not want to walk in Judea, because the Jews sought to kill Him. Now the Jews' Feast of Tabernacles was at hand." If you were studying this passage, one of the first questions you would ask is, "What is the Feast of Tabernacles?" By the way, the Jews who "sought to kill Him" were the religious leadership who, as a whole, categorically rejected Jesus' claim to be the Messiah from the very beginning of His public ministry. That didn't stop the Lord from teaching, as John 7:14 adds, "Now about the middle of the feast Jesus went up into the temple and taught."

We've unpacked the Feast of Tabernacles from Leviticus 23 earlier in our survey, but we didn't mention a first-century tradition that provided a powerful context for Jesus' teaching. While not mentioned in the Leviticus 23 passage, two significant traditions had developed which had become prominent in Jesus' day. One was called the "water pouring ceremony" which we discussed earlier in chapter 9. Remember, in the "water pouring ceremony," the priests brought water from the pool of Siloam and poured it onto the altar, praying for abundant rain that was needed for future harvests. Since Israel at that time was an agrarian society, rain was essential for survival; if they didn't get rains, they didn't get harvests. The water was a picture of God's blessing, God's provision, and God's presence.

The other prominent tradition that was part of the Sukkot celebration was called the "illumination of the temple." In the court of the women at the temple, there were four giant candelabras. The Talmud, the oral law in Judaism, notes that these candelabras were seventy-five feet tall. When they were lit at night, Jerusalem was illumined like it was the daytime. We don't know, because the New Testament doesn't specifically detail, but it may very well have been that Jesus was standing right next to these giant candelabras when He declared about Himself in John 8:12, "… I am the light of the world. He who follows Me shall not walk in darkness, but have the light of life."

Jesus and Hannukah. "Now it was the Feast of Dedication in Jerusalem, and it was winter. And Jesus walked in the temple, in Solomon's porch" (John 10:22–23). The **Feast of Dedication** is Hannukah. The word *Hanukkah* in Hebrew literally means "dedication." That's why it's called the Feast of Dedication.

Also known as the "Festival of Lights," Hannukah is an eight-day Jewish holiday commemorating the Jewish military victory by the Maccabees over the army of Seleucid king Antiochus and the rededication of the holy temple (the second temple) in Jerusalem at the time of the Maccabean Revolt of the second century B.C.

In 168 B.C., Antiochus sacrificed a pig on the holy altar, erected a seventy-five–foot–tall statue of himself, and demanded that the Jewish people worship him as "god." This began the revolt, which culminated three years later in 165 B.C. when the Maccabees defeated the army of Antiochus and cleansed and rededicated the temple to the Lord.

Jesus and Pentecost (Shavuot). In Acts 2, the birth of the church occurred on the Jewish feast of Shavuot, which we explored earlier. But there's much more here I want us to touch upon.

> When the Day of Pentecost had fully come, they were all with one accord in one place. And suddenly there came a sound from heaven, as of a rushing mighty wind, and it filled the whole house where they were sitting. Then there appeared to them divided tongues, as of fire, and one sat upon each of them. And they were all filled with the Holy Spirit and began to speak with other tongues, as the Spirit gave them utterance.
>
> —Acts 2:1–4

We know why the disciples were in Jerusalem for this feast day. In verses 2–4, there's some Old Testament context worth mentioning regarding the wind and tongues of fire. In Ezekiel 37, God promised to breathe life through the Spirit to dead bones—representing a spiritually dead Israel. When God gave Israel the law on Mt. Sinai in Exodus 19, He came down with a mighty sound and fire!

In verse 4, the Spirit fell on the believers. As we've learned, in the Old Testament the Spirit primarily empowered certain people for specific times and purposes (prophets, priests, kings, artisans). In the New Testament the Holy Spirit filled every believer in Messiah Jesus.

> And there were dwelling in Jerusalem Jews, devout men, from every nation under heaven. And when this sound occurred, the multitude came together, and were confused, because everyone heard them speak in his own language. Then they were all amazed and marveled, saying to one another, "Look, are not all these who speak Galileans? And how is it that we hear, each in our own language in which we were born? Parthians and Medes and Elamites, those dwelling in Mesopotamia, Judea and Cappadocia, Pontus and Asia, Phrygia and Pamphylia, Egypt and the parts of Libya adjoining Cyrene, visitors from Rome, both Jews and proselytes, Cretans and Arabs—we hear them speaking in our own tongues the wonderful works of God." So they were all amazed and perplexed, saying to one another, "Whatever could this mean?" Others mocking said, "They are full of new wine."
>
> —Acts 2:5–13

These disciples, simple Galileans, were speaking the wonderful works of God in the various languages of the day to people from all over the known world. Each person was hearing and understanding them in their own language. In the culture of that day, these Galileans would have been perceived as "local yokels" or "simpletons" by the audience, making this event even more remarkable. How did it happen? The disciples were filled and empowered by the Holy Spirit. In verses 14–17 in Acts 2, Peter provided perspective on the stunning developments of the day:

> But Peter, standing up with the eleven, raised his voice and said to them, "Men of Judea and all who dwell in Jerusalem, let this be known to you, and heed my words. For these are not drunk, as you suppose, since it is only the third hour of the day. But this is what was spoken by the prophet Joel: 'And it shall come to pass in the last days, says God, That I will pour out of My Spirit on all flesh; Your sons and your daughters shall prophesy, Your young men shall see visions, Your old men shall dream dreams.

Standing up with the eleven apostles, Peter addressed the men of Judea and the crowd. In verse 17 he said, "And it shall come to pass in the last days, says God, that I will pour out My Spirit on all flesh. ..." Peter was quoting from the Jewish prophet, Joel, who prophesied (Joel 2:28–29) a time when all those who followed God would receive His Spirit, not just prophets, priests, kings, and artisans. The "last days" refers to the present era of redemptive history from the first coming of Christ. This period will be completely fulfilled when Jesus returns at the Second Coming.

Incredibly, at Pentecost on the very birthday of the church, the great commission would come into focus as Jesus commanded, "Go therefore and make disciples of all the nations ..." (Matthew 28:19). Jesus had given marching orders just prior to His ascension earlier in Acts 1:8, "But you shall receive power when the Holy Spirit has come upon you; and you shall be witnesses to Me in Jerusalem, and in all Judea and Samaria, and to the end of the earth."

Peter continued in Acts 2:18 and following, and God provided a spiritual harvest of souls:

> Then Peter said to them, "Repent, and let every one of you be baptized in the name of Jesus Christ for the remission of sins; and you shall receive the gift of the Holy Spirit. For the promise is to you and to your children, and to all who are afar off, as many as the Lord our God will call." And with many other words he testified and exhorted them, saying, "Be saved from this perverse generation." Then those who gladly received his word were baptized; and that day about three thousand souls were added to them.
>
> —Acts 2:38–41

Many of those three thousand souls were visitors, Jewish people from all over the known world, and they would be returning home to tell others the good news about salvation found in Messiah Jesus.

It Is Written

In the New Testament we find the phrase "as it is written" about seventy times, depending upon the English translation. This phrase, sometimes overlooked and taken for granted, is important. But what does it mean, and why is it important?

The Old Testament, as we've come to understand, lays the foundation for the teachings, events, and truth found in the New Testament. The Bible is a progressive revelation. If you skip the first part of any good book and try to complete it, you'll have a difficult time understanding the characters, the plot, and the ending. In similar fashion, New Testament truth is best understood when we see its foundation in the events, characters, laws, sacrificial system, covenants, and promises of the Old Testament, as I trust you can attest.

How many times do the writers of the New Testament quote the Old Testament? An index in the Jewish New Testament catalogs 695 separate quotations from the books of the Old Testament in the New Testament.[21] There are many other passages where the Old Testament is referred to, as in cases where an Old Testament figure is mentioned, but no specific scripture is quoted. Depending on which scholar's work you examine, the total number of quotations, references, and allusions in the New Testament to the Old Testament may be as high as 4,105.[22]

New Testament authors, all Jewish with the possible exception of Luke, had knowledge of the Old Testament, from which quotations were drawn. They desired to communicate with and convince their fellow Jewish people that Jesus was the promised Messiah. They also wanted to communicate to all people everywhere that Jesus is God and the Savior of the world—that God's plan of redemption was not specifically for Jews or gentiles—it was for all humanity!

Anytime you read the phrase "as it is written," it's referring to an Old Testament text. For example, in Romans 3:10 we read, "As it is written, 'There is none righteous, no, not one.'" Here "it is written" refers to Ecclesiastes 7:20, which states, "For there is not a just man on earth who does good And does not sin." A study or reference Bible will typically have cross-references, enabling you to look up Old Testament scriptures that will deepen your understanding of

---

21. *Jewish New Testament Publications*, Jerusalem, 1989
22. Roger Nicole, *The Expositor's Bible Commentary*, Zondervan, Grand Rapids, 1979, Vol. I, p. 617

that particular New Testament text.

As we noted at the beginning of our study of the gospel near the beginning of our survey, when an individual in the New Testament makes reference to the "scriptures," it is in regard to the Old Testament. For instance, in Acts 17 we find the Apostle Paul testifying to the Bereans from the "scriptures" and the Bereans studying them also to test the authenticity of Paul's witness:

> Then Paul, as his custom was, went in to them, and for three Sabbaths **reasoned with them from the Scriptures,** explaining and demonstrating that the Christ had to suffer and rise again from the dead, and saying, "This Jesus whom I preach to you is the Christ." ... These were more fair-minded than those in Thessalonica, in that they received the word with all readiness, and **searched the Scriptures** daily to find out whether these things were so.
>
> —Acts 17:2–3, 11

Here are a few examples of Old Testament citations that amplify New Testament understanding:

Jesus came to fulfill the law and prophets. Jesus proclaimed this foundational truth in his first sermon, the Sermon on the Mount, in Matthew 5:17: "Do not think that I came to destroy the Law or the Prophets. I did not come to destroy but to fulfill." The "Law or the Prophets" refers to the entirety of the Old Testament. Jesus came to fulfill both messianic prophecy and the moral demands of the law in its entirety, for He was perfect—sinless.

In Matthew 5:18 the Lord added, "For assuredly, I say to you, till heaven and earth pass away, one jot or one tittle will by no means pass from the law till all is fulfilled." Jesus affirmed the authority of the Old Testament as God's Word. The "all" to be fulfilled are all the promises and prophecies in the Old Testament. In one sense, the implication is that our New Testament study will help us connect the dots of Jesus' life and teaching and gospel, which are initially concealed in the Old Testament, then revealed and fulfilled in the New Testament.

Jesus utilized the Old Testament in revealing His purpose and identity. In Luke 4:16–21 Jesus authenticated His messianic purpose and identity by reading about Himself in the synagogue from the scriptures:

> So He came to Nazareth, where He had been brought up. And as His custom was, He went into the synagogue on the Sabbath day, and stood up to read. And He was handed the book of the prophet Isaiah. And when He had opened the book, He found the place where it was written: "The Spirit of the Lord is upon Me, Because He has anointed Me To preach the gospel to the poor; He has sent Me to heal the brokenhearted, To proclaim liberty to the captives And recovery of sight to the blind, To set at liberty those who are oppressed; To proclaim the acceptable year of the Lord." Then He closed the book, and gave it back to the attendant and sat down. And the eyes of all who were in the synagogue were fixed on Him. And He began to say to them, "Today this Scripture is fulfilled in your hearing."

In this Luke 4 passage, Jesus was quoting from Isaiah 61:1–2. Notice the crux of his reading— "Today this Scripture is fulfilled in your hearing." His claim to be the Messiah was crystal clear!

Hopefully you have gleaned with clarity increased understanding of the gospel and personal work of Jesus through our biblical survey of redemptive history from Genesis to Revelation.

Some Closing Thoughts

If you have trusted in Jesus as your Lord and Savior, I trust this book has strengthened your faith and deepened your understanding of the gospel.

If you've not yet trusted in Jesus, yet believe the message proclaimed throughout this book, that Jesus is the Lamb of God, who died for your sins and rose again from the dead, I plead with you—be reconciled to God. Confess your sins to God and turn from them, which is to repent. Then tell the Lord you believe that Jesus died for you and rose again. Ask Him to forgive your sins, and by faith, receive Him as your Lord and Savior. When you do, let a Christian in your life know of your decision. You may also feel free to contact me as you begin walking with the Lord.

For you who know Christ, we've spent much time talking about the idea of harvest, both the physical and spiritual. I want to encourage you by pointing to the agricultural nature of our salvation, our daily walk with God, and our future glory in heaven.

Our salvation: Notice the agricultural idea of the new birth, as Peter described God's Word as imperishable seed in 1 Peter 1:23, "having been born again, not of corruptible seed but incorruptible, through the word of God which lives and abides forever."

Our walk with God: In Psalm 1:3 scripture compares a person who follows God's Word to a healthy flourishing plant, "He shall be like a tree Planted by the rivers of water, That brings forth its fruit in its season, Whose leaf also shall not wither; And whatever he does shall prosper."

Our future home in heaven: The book of Revelation ties

together the images of greenery and fruitfulness with the consummation of our redemption in Christ. In the new heavens and new earth, we find the tree of life from the Garden of Eden!!

The fruitfulness of the land of Israel celebrated at Pentecost not only pictured God's present goodness, but for the believer, also points forward to the fruitfulness of the new heavens and earth. As Revelation 22:1–2 states, "And he showed me a pure river of water of life, clear as crystal, proceeding from the throne of God and of the Lamb. In the middle of its street, and on either side of the river, was the tree of life, which bore twelve fruits, each tree yielding its fruit every month. The leaves of the tree were for the healing of the nations."

Therefore—remember, rejoice, anticipate, and occupy until He returns—offering ourselves and the firstfruits of our lives—our time, talent, and resources for the building of His church and glorification of His Name.

The literal, physical return of Jesus should always be close to our hearts as our blessed hope and an urgent impetus for bold proclamation and intensive disciple making. To borrow the words from one Bible teacher: "While we look forward to the end time, we continue to tarry and work in the meantime! In other words, fix our eyes on Jesus, but at the same time strive to make disciples."

Just like sowing seed and working a field in the physical world requires faith and trust for God to provide the blessing, so it is in the spiritual world! God is faithful! Hallelujah! Maranatha!

Chapter 12 Study Guide

1. What is the general context for better understanding of the New Testament text?
2. As mentioned in our study, the death and resurrection of Jesus occur in the context of Passover, as He is the "Lamb of God who takes away the sin of the world." Which gospels contain information about the ministry of Jesus during Passover time?
3. How much content in the Gospel of John is directly associated with the ministry of Christ during "Passion Week," the week of Passover? What specific events in the life of Christ are recorded in the Gospel of John during this time?
4. Where in the Gospel of John was Jesus teaching during the Feast of Tabernacles? What two ceremonies or traditions were observed in Jesus' day at the temple, and how does He use them as backdrops to teach gospel truth about Himself?
5. What is the Feast of Dedication in John 10:22–23? Give a brief explanation of this feast. How do you think the concept of dedication applies, in general, to the Christian life?
6. We've learned that the birth of the church in Acts 2, Pentecost, occurred on the Jewish Feast day of Shavuot. What made this particular Shavuot so unique for the disciples and the people present on that eventful day?
7. When Peter preached to the crowd in Acts 2, what material did he use in Acts 2:16–21, Acts 2:25–28, and Acts 2:34–35?
8. What does the phrase "it is written" usually refer to in the New Testament? How may this recognition be utilized in Bible study?
9. What are some overall takeaways you've gleaned from our Jewish roots study, surveying redemptive history from Genesis to Revelation?

10. How has your relationship with the Lord grown as a result of this endeavor in God's Word?

About The Author

Christianity Is Jewish!

I know, I know! I'm stating the obvious! Or perhaps that was a revelation to you prior to reading this book. Whatever your response to that statement, know that my views about that statement have changed dramatically. At one point it was completely irrelevant. Today, that comment plays a major role in who I am as a human being.

Growing up in a Reform Jewish home in St. Pete, Florida, I attended synagogue, and at age thirteen went through Bar-Mitzvah which means "son of the commandment" and is a ceremonial rite of passage when a Jewish boy becomes a man. Though we were culturally and socially very connected to the Jewish community, we were not a particularly religious household.

Growing up, I believed in God as far back as I can remember and had some sense that He knew me. In high school I sought fulfillment in athletics and academics, as I was a state-ranked tennis player in Florida and an honors student. But accomplishment didn't fulfill the longings of my soul.

In college at the University of Florida I got involved in the party scene. This didn't satisfy me either. In fact, I was that young person walking in quiet desperation—empty and walking without a plan for life.

My earliest memories of people sharing Jesus with me go back to my college years. But, I consistently rejected any conversation about Jesus and turned down invitations to church, Bible studies, and Christian concerts. Then a good friend, Greg, a Christian, challenged me. He said, "Do you know who you are and do you know where you're going when you die?" I had no idea how to answer those questions. In fact, they sent me into an existential crisis of sorts. God used that crisis as a catalyst, as I began searching for truth in 1985.

At that time, I embraced neither my Judaism nor any other religion, but began to examine different philosophies and world religions for answers to life's biggest questions.

I searched for something I could believe in, something that would fill a void I felt in my life that accomplishment or earthly pleasures could not fill. My search culminated in the fall of 1987 when a stranger on a plane challenged me to ask the God of Israel if Jesus is the Messiah. I took his challenge, crying out to God as I knew Him to show me the truth about Jesus.

He did, and in December 1987 I trusted in Jesus. I believed for the first time that He died for my sins and rose again from the dead so that I could be forgiven. Knowing Messiah was and is the greatest thing that's ever happened in my life, but it's not easy being a Jew for Jesus.

Something profound occurred in my life as a new Christian: I made a discovery that was quite astonishing to me at the time. As I began studying the New Testament, I learned about the Jewishness of Jesus. I also learned all the writers of the New Testament were Jewish with the possible exception of Luke. I thought to myself, "Christianity is Jewish!"

In one sense the gospel narrative is simply a Jewish debate among Jewish people about the true identity of a Jewish man, Jesus. And the story takes place in Israel. What could be more Jewish than that?

The Impact of the Holocaust

My father and his family immigrated from Bonn, Germany in June 1939, escaping Nazi persecution. My paternal grandparents and my young father escaped with help from an SS Agent in the Nazi party. The agent, a friend of my grandfather's from WWI, falsified immigration papers enabling my father and his parents to escape to Belize, where they lived for two years before moving to Daytona Beach in 1941. None of my father's remaining family in Germany survived the holocaust.

Professional Tennis Coaching

I picked up my first tennis racquet at the age of 9 and from the ages of 12 to 18 I competed in the Florida junior circuit, earning my highest state ranking of #20 in the boys 16-under singles division. It was my main sport, though I loved playing many sports. After graduating from the University of Florida in 1986, I began coaching under my high school coach, Billy Stearns, at his academy in Seminole, Florida. I trained world-class juniors, college and professional tennis players. During my 20s and 30s, I was a professional tennis coach who loved my outdoor "office" and working with people. I came to East Tennessee to pursue my Master's Degree in 1991, and joined the coaching staff at East Tennessee State University under Head Coach Dave Mullins. Coach and I worked together for nine years, and I taught private lessons and clinics on the side with a faithful client base.

Stepping Away from the Racquet

As I grew as a Christian, my desire to share this good news with my

Jewish people also grew. I wanted them to know that yes, it is Jewish to believe in Jesus, for He is the Jewish Messiah and Savior of the world. I prayed for God to make an opportunity for me to share the gospel with fellow Jews. In 1989 a family friend passed on a pamphlet from Jews for Jesus, a missionary society committed to sharing Messiah with the Jewish people. Before receiving this newsletter I thought I was alone, the only Jew who believed in Jesus.

After a few years of receiving the newsletter, I decided to serve for a six-week summer outreach with Jews for Jesus. In the process of applying, I learned about The Liberated Wailing Wall, Jews for Jesus' mobile evangelistic music team. This team shared the good news of Jesus through music, drama, and testimony, mainly at churches and at Christian colleges. They also would engage in street evangelism in big cities and on college campuses. After much consideration and prayer, I went ahead and applied for the music team as well.

In the plan of God, a six-week short-term mission trip turned into a two-year full-time ministry commitment. In June of 1997, I left Johnson City, Tennessee with no more than a book bag, a twenty-nine—inch hard-shell suitcase, and a guitar. Everything else I left in storage. I boarded an airplane, flew away and entered a life-changing adventure!

In December of 1997, before my team left for our tour of ministry, we recorded a messianic praise album called, This is Jerusalem.

In January 1998, my team of six members and I loaded our gear onto a forty-foot fully-equipped tour bus, which became our home on the road. I co-led the traveling music team on our journey around the United States and Canada from January 1998 to March 1999. At the end of our North American tour, we embarked on a two-month world tour doing ministry in England, South Africa, Australia, and Hawaii.

Needless to say, after doing over 500 presentations in a myriad of diverse church settings and evangelizing around the world, my life was forever changed. During my tour, I courted a beautiful woman named Lori, and at the end of the tour I asked her to be my wife. We were married in the fall of 1999 and two years later God blessed us with our firstborn son, Elijah.

Ministry in the Big Apple

In 2002, I was accepted onto vocational missionary staff with Jews for Jesus. My family and I packed up our house and moved to New York City in January of 2003. Arriving in the Big Apple, we moved into our apartment in midtown Manhattan. Shortly after arriving in New York City, Lori and I learned that we were expecting our second child, a daughter.

In Manhattan, I trained under some of the brightest and most gifted missionaries and Bible teachers including the late Dr. Jhan Moskowitz, who taught me much about preaching, and Dr. Jack Meadows, my private theology professor. Following the training, I was ordained, and then continued on as a missionary in the heart of New York City through mid-2009.

Pastoral Service

Grace Fellowship in Johnson City, TN has been the most influential church in my Christian life. It was there I learned to function in a local body of believers. The church supported and sent me out on both my two-year and six-year missionary stints with Jews for Jesus. Just prior to leaving for New York City in January 2003, I sat under staff pastor Tim Bowers in a six month resident's program where my main responsibilities included developing a seeker-sensitive, gospel-centered Bible study.

After leaving staff with Jews for Jesus in 2009, I served as Missionary-in-Residence for a year before becoming the full-time Local Outreach Pastor. During my service at Grace Fellowship from 2009–2013, I developed and directed various community outreach programs and mission activities, trained missions teams, taught classes and preached on a number of occasions.

Larry Stamm Ministries

I am a Jewish Christian in love with Jesus the Messiah and the Word of God. God's work in my life to this point prepared me to launch Larry Stamm Ministries in early 2013 with the full support of our Board of Directors, my family, and my home church. My experience since 1997 in witnessing around the globe to people of all walks of life has uniquely qualified me to teach and share biblical principles with others and to help them share their faith more confidently.

More and more Americans are avoiding the church and an increasing number of both irreligious and religiously unaffiliated no longer have friends who are Christians. We can't afford to isolate ourselves, or to stop reaching out to our co-workers, neighbors, classmates, and others. The onus is ever more upon individual Christians to share Jesus in the marketplace: at the coffee shop, with your neighbor or coworker, your classmates and others with whom you have everyday contact.

Larry Stamm Ministries exists to make the gospel of Jesus a confident topic of conversation for every Christian. We provide classes, one-on-one evangelism coaching and teaching that connects the dots between the Old and New Testaments to inspire Christians to press on in fulfilling the Great Commission.

Connect With Larry

Larry Stamm Ministries
Post Office Box 1072   Jonesborough, TN 37659
Phone: 423-406-2066
E-mail: lsministries@outlook.com
Website: larrystamm.org
Facebook: @ "Larry Stamm Ministries"
Vimeo Video Channel:
https://vimeo.com/channels/larrystammministries

Bibliography

The Real Kosher Jesus by Dr. Michael Brown

Christ in the Passover by Moishe and Ceil Rosen

Christ in the Feast of Pentecost by David Brickner and Rich Robinson

The Fall Feasts of Israel by Mitch and Zhava Glazer

Israel, the Land, and the People; H. Wayne House – General Editor

Rose Guide to The Temple by Randall Price (Rose Publishing)

Unholy War by Randall Price

Our Hands Are Stained with Blood by Dr. Michael Brown